DISCOVERING AMERICA

Upper Atlantic

NEW JERSEY • NEW YORK

By
Thomas G. Aylesworth
Virginia L. Aylesworth

CHELSEA HOUSE PUBLISHERS
New York • Philadelphia

First Printing

1   3   5   7   9   8   6   4   2

Library of Congress Cataloging-in-Publication Data

Aylesworth, Thomas G.
    Upper Atlantic: New Jersey, New York
Thomas G. Aylesworth, Virginia L. Aylesworth.
        p. cm.—(Discovering America)
    Includes bibliographical references and index.
    Summary: Discusses the geographical, historical, and cultural aspects of
New Jersey and New York. Includes maps, illustrated fact spreads, and
other relevant material.
    ISBN 0-7910-3399-6.
        0-7910-3417-8 (pbk.)
    1. Middle Atlantic States—Juvenile literature. 2. New Jersey—Juvenile literature. 3. New York
(State)—Juvenile literature. [1. Middle Atlantic States. 2. New Jersey. 3. New York (State)]
I. Aylesworth, Virginia L. II. Title. III. Series: Aylesworth, Thomas G. Discovering America.

F106.A98   1995   94-45826
974.7—dc20   CIP
                                                   AC

CONTENTS

NEW YORK 33

New Jersey

   The great seal of New Jersey was adopted in 1776 and the design amended in 1928. The shield in the center shows three plows and the goddess Ceres holding a horn of plenty, to represent the state's agriculture, and the figure of Liberty. Above the shield is a sovereign's helmet and a horse's head. Below is a scroll with the state motto and the date 1776, the year the state signed the Declaration of Independence.

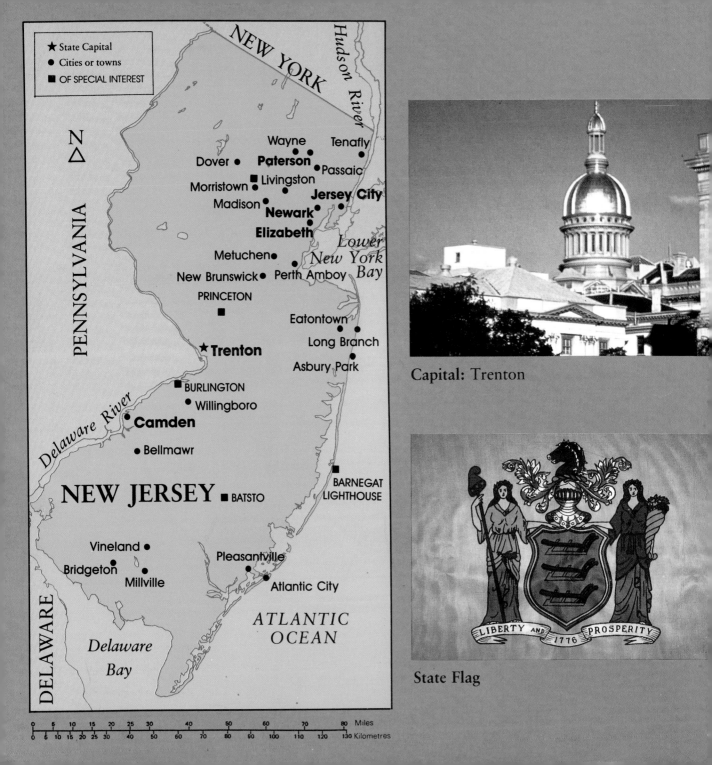

Map Legend

★ State Capital
● Cities or towns
■ OF SPECIAL INTEREST

N

NEW YORK

Hudson River

PENNSYLVANIA

Wayne
Tenafly
Dover
Paterson
Passaic
Morristown
Livingston
Jersey City
Madison
Newark
Elizabeth
Metuchen
Lower New York Bay
New Brunswick
Perth Amboy
PRINCETON
Eatontown
★ **Trenton**
Long Branch
Asbury Park
BURLINGTON
Willingboro
Camden
Bellmawr

Delaware River

NEW JERSEY
■ BATSTO
■ BARNEGAT LIGHTHOUSE

Vineland
Bridgeton
Millville
Pleasantville
Atlantic City

DELAWARE

Delaware Bay

ATLANTIC OCEAN

| 0 | 5 | 10 | 15 | 20 | 25 | 30 | 40 | 50 | 60 | 70 | 80 Miles |
| 0 | 6 | 10 | 15 | 20 | 25 | 30 | 40 | 50 | 60 | 70 | 80 | 90 | 100 | 110 | 120 | 130 Kilometres |

Capital: Trenton

State Flag

LIBERTY AND 1776 PROSPERITY

NEW JERSEY
At a Glance

Major Industries: Manufacturing, chemicals, petroleum
Major Crops: Hay, corn, soybeans, truck crops

Size: 7,787 square miles (46th largest)
Population: 7,789,060 (9th largest)

State Motto: Liberty and Prosperity
State Tree: Red Oak
Nickname: The Garden State

State Flower: Violet
State Bird: Eastern Goldfinch

State Flag
In 1896 New Jersey adopted its flag, which carries the state seal (basically Jersey blue) on a buff-colored background.

State Motto
Liberty and Prosperity
This motto was adopted in 1928; it expresses both patriotism and hope for the future.

The Cape May County Park, in Cape May, has a large lake, rides, and a petting zoo.

State Capital

In British colonial times, when New Jersey was divided into eastern and western sections, there were two capitals—Perth Amboy and Burlington. This split lasted from 1676 to 1775. From 1775 to 1790 there was no definite capital. Since 1790 the capital has been Trenton.

State Name and Nicknames

In 1664 the English took over from the Dutch the territory that was to become New Jersey. John, Lord Berkeley and Sir George Carteret were named Lord Proprietors of the area. Carteret had been born on the Isle of Jersey in the English Channel and had been the governor there, so the new British territory was named "New Jersey."

New Jersey is called the *Garden State* because of the numerous truck farms that supply so much produce for the region. The state has other nicknames, too. Because of the shellfish found off the coast, it has been called the *Clam State*. Some other nicknames were the *Camden and Amboy State* (for the railroad that crossed the area), the *Jersey Blue State* (for the colony's Revolutionary War uniforms), and the *Pathway of the Revolution* (for the important battles fought there during the American Revolution).

State Flower

Viola sororia—the common purple, or meadow, violet—was adopted as the state flower of New Jersey in 1913. In 1971 it was made official by a legislative act that took effect the next year.

State Trees

New Jersey has not only a state tree but also a state memorial tree. The state tree is the northern red oak, *Quercus rubra*, and was selected in 1950. In 1951 the legislature adopted the flowering dogwood tree, *Cornus florida*, as the state memorial tree.

State Bird

The eastern goldfinch, *Spinus tristis tristis*, was selected by the New Jersey legislature as the state bird in 1935.

State Animal

The horse was adopted as the state animal in 1977. The racing industry and the number of horse farms in the state are impressive and greatly contribute to the state's economy.

State Insect

Because of its economic importance to the state, the honeybee, *Apis mellifera*, was named the state insect in 1974.

Population

The population of New Jersey in 1992 was 7,789,060, making it the ninth most populous state. There are 1,049 people per square mile—making New Jersey second only to Washington, D.C., in population density.

Industries

The principal industry of New Jersey is manufacturing. The chief products are chemicals, electronic and electrical equipment, nonelectrical machinery, and fabricated metals. New Jersey is also home to many service- and trade-oriented industries. In 1992 tourism brought in $17.9 billion. Gambling in Atlantic City is also a source of much income.

Agriculture

The chief crops of the state are hay, corn, soybeans, tomatoes, blueberries, peaches, and cranberries. New Jersey is also a livestock state, and there are estimated to be some 77,000 cattle; 24,000 hogs and pigs; 13,000 sheep; and 2.1 million chickens, geese, and turkeys on its farms. Pine, cedar, and hardwood timber are harvested; and crushed stone, sand, and gravel are important mineral products. Commercial fishing brings in some $96.9 million a year.

Government

The governor of New Jersey holds the only executive office in the state. The state legislature, which meets annually, consists of a 29-member senate and a 60-member general assembly, with each county electing one to four senators and one to nine assemblymen, depending on their populations. Senators serve four-year terms and assemblymen are elected biennially. The most recent state constitution was adopted in 1947. In addition to its two U.S. senators, New Jersey has 14 representatives in the House of Representatives. The state has 16 votes in the electoral college.

Sports

New Jersey has always been a hotbed of sports activity. The first game in organized baseball was played in Hoboken in 1846, when the New York Nine beat the New York Knickerbockers 23-1. In 1869 Rutgers beat Princeton 6-4 in New Brunswick in the world's first intercollegiate football game. In 1970, American of Wayne, New Jersey, won the Little League World Series. Then another New Jersey Little League team, Lakewood, took the title in 1975. In professional sports, two New York teams, the Jets and Giants of the

The Giants of the NFL play at the Meadowlands.

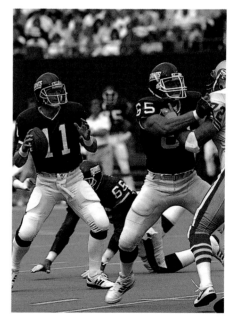

National Football League, play at Giants Stadium in the Meadowlands Sports Complex, and the Nets of the National Basketball Association and the Devils of the National Hockey League play at the Meadowlands Arena.

Major Cities
Atlantic City (population 37,986). Settled in 1852, Atlantic City soon became the best known of New Jersey's beach resorts. At first it was a honeymoon haven for newlyweds. Then, with the construction of Convention Hall—the largest hall east of the Mississippi—it became a favorite place for conventioneers and the home of the Miss America Pageant. Today, with its legalized gambling, Atlantic City is the mecca for some 19 million visitors every year.

A 60-foot-wide boardwalk runs the 5-mile length of the beach, and the city boasts the first pedestrian mall in the state—Gordon's Alley.

There is also the Edwin B. Forsythe National Wildlife Refuge, Brigantine Division, which includes nature trails, observation blinds, and a wilderness area. Other places to visit in Atlantic City include the Shops on Ocean One, Garden Pier, the Historic Towne of Smithville, Storybookland, and the Noyes Museum.

Atlantic City is the city on which the popular board game Monopoly was based.
Camden (population 87,492). Settled in 1681, Camden became a leading industrial, marketing, and transportation center before the Civil War. The great American poet Walt Whitman spent the last 20 years of his life here. Visitors can tour the only home he ever owned, at 330 Mickle Street—the Walt Whitman House State Historic Site—and his tomb in Harleigh Cemetery. Also open to the public are Pomona Hall, a Georgian house dating from 1726, and

the Campbell Museum, with its collection of 18th- and 19th-century silver and porcelain soup tureens, bowls, and ladles.
Elizabeth (population 110,002). Settled in 1664, Elizabeth was a thriving industrial town. What is now Princeton University was founded in Elizabeth in 1746 as the College of New Jersey. The Boxwood Hall State Historic Site is also located here. Elizabeth was the home of Elias Boudinot, who was president of the Continental Congress in 1783 and who later became director of the United States Mint.
Jersey City (population 228,517). Settled in 1629, Jersey City grew as a manufacturing and transportation center largely because of its location on the Hudson River due west of the southern tip of Manhattan Island. There are almost 600 industrial plants in this, New Jersey's second largest city. Liberty State Park is nearby, giving

visitors a breathtaking view of the Manhattan skyline as well as ferry service to the Statue of Liberty and Ellis Island.

Newark (population 275,221). Settled in 1666, Newark is the most populous city in New Jersey and one of the leading manufacturing cities in the world. The Old Plume House, which is now a church rectory, is believed to have been built in 1710. Newark's Cathedral of the Sacred Heart resembles the cathedral in Reims, France. In 1967 Newark was the site of race riots that attracted attention to its housing and economic problems. Similar riots erupted elsewhere in the United States. Newark International Airport is one of the busiest in the world; the port of Newark is one of the busiest in the nation and is a major port of entry for foreign cars and a main carrier of containerized freight.

Paterson (population 140,891). Settled in 1711,

Paterson began to become an industrial city when Alexander Hamilton saw the possibility of harnessing the Great Falls of the Passaic River for industrial purposes. The Great Falls Historic District contains High Falls and a renovated railway system. Lambert Castle was built in 1893 by Catholina Lambert, an immigrant who became rich in the silk manufacturing business.

Trenton (population 88,675). Settled in 1679, Trenton became the state capital in 1790. Washington attacked the British-held town of Trenton after crossing the Delaware River near Trenton on December 26, 1776. Today Trenton is the site of some 400 manufacturing plants. Visitors can tour the State House and the State Museum. The Old Barracks museum was built in 1758–59 and housed British, Hessian, and Continental troops during the Revolution. The oldest

house in Trenton is the William Trent House (1719).

Places To Visit
The National Park Service maintains four areas in the state of New Jersey: Morristown National Historical Park; part of the Delaware Water Gap National Recreation Area; the Sandy Hook Unit of Gateway National Recreation Area; and Edison National Historic Site. In addition, there are 32 state recreation areas.

Allaire State Park: Historic Allaire Village. In this old workers' town are several buildings dating back to 1853.
Bernardsville: Great Swamp National Wildlife Refuge. More than 200 species of animals live in the 6,800-acre refuge.
Bordentown: Clara Barton Schoolhouse. Barton, founder of the American Red Cross, established one of the country's first free schools here in 1851.
Branchville: Space Farms Zoo & Museum.
Bridgeton: Gibbon House. This was the site of a pre-

Revolution tea-burning party protesting King George III's taxes.

Caldwell: Grover Cleveland Birthplace State Historic Site. Cleveland, both the 22nd and 24th president of the United States, was born and raised in this house, built in 1832.

Cherry Hill: Barclay Farmstead. One of the earliest properties in the area, Barclay Farmstead includes restored farm buildings dating to 1684.

Clark: Dr. William Robinson Plantation Museum. The museum contains a 1690 farmhouse and outbuildings.

Clinton: Clinton Historical Museum Village. A 1763 mill and old shops and stores recreate New Jersey's past.

Flemington: Black River & Western Railroad. Excursion rides to Ringoes and back are available on an old steam train.

Freehold: Covenhoven House. This 18th-century house was occupied by British General Henry Clinton before the Battle of Monmouth in 1778.

Gibbstown: Nothnagle House. This is the oldest log house in the United States, built in 1638.

Hackensack: The Church on the Green. Built in 1696, this Dutch Reformed church is one of the oldest in the state.

Jackson: Six Flags Great Adventure. An amusement park that also has a drive-through safari park on its 1,100 acres.

Margate: Lucy the Elephant. This six-story Victorian folly, built in the shape of an elephant, was once a seaside hotel.

Millville: Victorian Wheaton Village. A reconstructed glassmaking town, Wheaton Village features a working glass factory and other buildings.

Montclair: Israel Crane House. Dating back to 1796, the Israel Crane House is a large mansion in the Federalist style.

Morristown: Historic Speedwell. This is the home and factory of Stephen Vail, where the engine for the *Savannah*, the first steamship to cross the Atlantic, was built in 1838. Samuel F.B. Morse also perfected and tested the electric telegraph here.

Morristown National Historical Park: Created in 1933, this park contains a

George Washington's headquarters at the Morristown Historical Park.

museum, the Ford Mansion (1774), Fort Nonsense (1777), Wick House, and Jockey Hollow (the winter headquarters of the Continental Army from 1779 to 1780).

New Brunswick: Buccleuch Mansion. Dating from 1739, the mansion contains period rooms.

Plainfield: Drake House Museum. Now the Plainfield Historical Society headquarters, it was

George Washington's headquarters in 1777.

Princeton: Nassau Hall. On the campus of Princeton University, the Second Continental Congress met here in 1783. Rockingham State Historic Site. This was Washington's headquarters in 1783, where he wrote his "Farewell Orders to the Armies."

Ringwood State Park: Ringwood Manor. Originally, the home of a succession of ironmasters, including Robert Erskine, Surveyor General of the Continental Army, the house contains a collection of fine furniture.

Salem: Hancock House. Dating from 1734, the building housed 30 volunteer Quakers guarding the nearby drawbridge during the Revolution.

Short Hills: Cora Hartshorn Arboretum and Bird Sanctuary. This 17-acre park has nature trails and a museum with nature exhibits.

Somerville: Wallace House State Historic Site. Built in 1778, the house was Washington's headquarters.

Stanhope: Waterloo Village Restoration. Waterloo Village flourished as a cargo and transshipment center during the heyday of the Morris Canal until the railroad bypassed it in 1881.

Wayne: Dey Mansion. Built about 1740, this house was Washington's headquarters in 1780.

West Orange: Edison National Historic Site. Built in 1887, the main building was used by the inventor as his headquarters for 44 years, and contains his laboratory and workshops.

Events

Here are some of the events scheduled in New Jersey.

Sports: Jersey Coast Boat Show (Asbury Park), horse racing at Monmouth Park (Asbury Park), National Bocce Tournament (Asbury Park), horse racing at Atlantic City Race Course (Atlantic City), Cowtown Rodeo (Deepwater), harness racing at Freehold Raceway (Freehold), baseball card convention (Ocean City).

Arts and Crafts: Boardwalk Art and Craft Show (Atlantic City), Indian Summer Boardwalk Art and Craft Show (Atlantic City), Peters Valley Crafts Fair (Branchville), Wood Street Fair (Burlington), Promenade Art Exhibit (Cape May), Flower Show (Ocean City), Boardwalk Arts Show (Ocean City).

Music: Concerts at the Riverfront (Bridgeton), Concerts at the Garden State Arts Center (Matawan), New Jersey Symphony Orchestra (Newark and elsewhere), New Jersey State Opera (Newark), Concerts (Ocean City), Outdoor Concerts (Somerville).

Entertainment: Miss America Pageant (Atlantic City), State Fair (Cherry Hill), Six Flags Great Adventure (Jackson), Action Park (McAfee), Middlesex County Fair (New Brunswick), Night in Venice (Ocean City), Hermit Crab Race (Ocean City), Festival of the Sea (Point Pleasant Beach), Wings 'n' Water Festival (Stone Harbor), Reenactment of Crossing of the Delaware (Trenton).

Theater: Summer Theatre (Glassboro), Starlight Summer Theater (Long Beach Island), New Jersey Shakespeare Festival Theatre (Madison), Paper Mill Playhouse (Millburn), Summerfun Summer Theater (Montclair), Theater of Universal Images (Newark), George Street Playhouse (New Brunswick).

Above:
The Atlantic Coastal Plain is characterized by long, flat lowland and is most prevalent in the southern half of the state.

At right:
Atlantic City, located on the southern coast, is one of the busiest resort towns in the Northeast. Hotels and casinos are among the most popular features of Atlantic City, the only area in the country besides Nevada where organized gambling is legal.

Below:
A beach in Atlantic City near the famous Boardwalk.

Dairy farms are a common sight in the Delaware Water Gap region.

The Land and the Climate

The Garden State is often thought of as a state filled with factories, oil refineries, research laboratories, and industrial towns. But those are confined mainly to a 15-mile-wide corridor that stretches westward from Newark to Camden on the border. The rest of the state is filled with natural beauty. There are 200-year-old towns with tree-shaded streets. There are more than 800 lakes and ponds, 100 rivers and creeks, and 1400 miles of streams. Add to that 127 miles of beaches stretching from Sandy Hook in northern New Jersey to Cape May in the south. New Jersey as a whole is a state of great variety.

18

A general store built around the time of the Revolution.

Most of New Jersey is surrounded by water. Its more than 127 miles of beaches are among the most popular in the region.

Except for a 48-mile land border with New York in the north, New Jersey is surrounded by water. The Hudson River and the Atlantic Ocean are on the east. Delaware Bay is on the southwest. And the Delaware River is on the west. Most of the state's soil, except for the salt marshes and sandy areas along the Atlantic Coast, is ideal for farming.

New Jersey has four main land regions. In the northeast is the Appalachian Ridge and Valley Region, part of a mountainous area that runs from New York to Alabama. High Point, the state's highest peak, rises 1,803 feet here. It is part of the Kittatinny Mountains, New Jersey's chief mountain range. The Delaware Water Gap, formed where the Delaware River cuts through the mountains, is located in this region; it is one of the most beautiful areas in the East. Apples and vegetables are the main crops in this part of the state, and herds of dairy cattle graze on the picturesque grassy slopes of the valleys.

The New England Upland, sometimes called the Highlands, is southeast of the Appalachian Ridge and Valley Region. Much of this area is covered with flat-topped ridges of hard rock. But the Highlands are also filled with lovely lakes, which attract sportsmen from all over for fishing, boating, and swimming.

The Piedmont crosses the top half of New Jersey northeast to southwest. It is only about 20 miles wide and covers some 20 percent of the state. But almost 75 percent of the people in the Garden State live here. Most of them are in industrial cities like Elizabeth, Jersey City, and Paterson. The reason for this concentration of industry is that so many of the state's rivers are found here, and in the early days before the railroads, goods and manufactured items had to be carried by boat. Among these rivers are the Hudson, the Musconetcong, the Passaic, the Ramapo, and the Raritan.

The rest of the state, south of the Piedmont, is called the Atlantic Coastal Plain. In most places this gently rolling lowland is less than 100 feet above sea level. Truck farms, those farms on which vegetables are grown for the markets, work the fertile soil of the west and southwest parts of this area. At the western edge of the plain are Camden, Trenton, and other cities that lie along the wide Delaware River. In the eastern portion of the Atlantic Coastal Plain there are forests and salt marshes. Since the soil here is rather poor, large portions of this area are thinly populated. But the Atlantic coast has more than 50 resort cities and towns such as Atlantic City, Asbury Park, and Cape May.

A long, narrow sandbar runs along most of the state's 130-mile Atlantic coastline. There are many inlets through this sandbar, which have formed bays between the bar and the mainland. From north to south, the bays are Newark Bay, Raritan Bay, Sandy Hook Bay, Barnegat Bay, Little Egg Harbor, Great Bay, and Great Egg Bay. The coastal regions of New Jersey are among the most popular vacation areas in the United States.

Because of the ocean breezes, the eastern coast of the state has a mild climate—cool in summer and warm in winter. The average January temperatures range from 34 degrees F. in the south to 26 degrees F. in the northwest. Average July temperatures range from 76 degrees F. in the southwest to 70 degrees F. in the north. However, because of its long coastline, New Jersey is susceptible to violent storms sweeping in from the Atlantic Ocean.

Many farms in southern New Jersey grow vegetables that provide the markets in the region with fresh produce.

A "false face" mask, made by one of the tribes of the Iroquois, the Indian nation that ranged across the eastern United States.

The History

There were probably about 8,000 Indians living in what is now New Jersey before the European settlers arrived. They were peaceful Native Americans who called themselves Leni-Lenape—"The Original People." They spent most of their time hunting, but they also raised maize (or corn), beans, squash, and other crops. When white settlers came, they called these Indians of the Algonkian family the Delawares, after their home valley.

Probably the first European to explore the New Jersey coast was Giovanni da Verrazano, an Italian navigator in the service of France, who reached the area in 1524. In 1609 Henry Hudson, an English sea captain employed by the Dutch, explored the area around Sandy Hook Bay and sailed up the river that bears his name. Cornelius Mey, a Dutch explorer, sailed the Delaware River in 1614—Cape May was later named for him. Mey was the founder of Fort Nassau, near the site of today's Glouster City. By 1618 the Dutch had established a trading post at Bergen, and about 1630 they set up another outpost at Pavonia, which is now a part of Jersey City. There were also small Swedish settlements on the Delaware and Maurice Rivers. Still, the Indians had the land pretty much to themselves.

Because they feared Swedish competition in the fur trade, the Dutch forced the Swedes out of New Jersey in 1655. The first permanent settlement in New Jersey was probably that of Bergen, a fortified town that is now also a part of Jersey City.

Then came a change of power. In 1644 Charles II of England granted his brother James, the Duke of York, extensive New World holdings, including what later became known as New Jersey. James, in turn, gave the land to two of his friends, Lord John Berkeley and Sir George Carteret. The Dutch gave up their claim to the area without a fight, and the two Englishmen sold the land to settlers at low prices. One important decision made by Berkeley and Carteret was to allow religious and political freedom in their territory. It was a daring idea for the time, but welcome news to oppressed minorities. Soon people were arriving in droves.

Carteret had been something of a hero in the defense of the Isle of Jersey, one of the English Channel islands off the northwest coast of France. Thus it was he who named the new territory New Jersey.

English colonization progressed rapidly, as Calvinists, Congregationalists, and Presbyterians moved in to civilize the eastern half of the area. In 1674 a group of Quakers, headed by Edward Billynge, bought Berkeley's holdings in the western half of the territory. Two years later, in 1676, the colony was divided into two sections—West Jersey and East Jersey.

When Queen Anne came to the English throne in 1702, she demanded that all the proprietors surrender their rights of government to England. The halves of New Jersey were united into a single royal province. Still, from 1703 to 1775, the colony had two capitals. They were Perth Amboy, the former capital of East Jersey, and Burlington, the former capital of West Jersey. At first, the governor of New York also ruled New Jersey. But the settlers protested, and in 1738 England gave New Jersey its own governor, Lewis Morris.

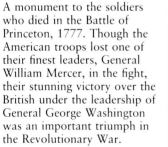

A monument to the soldiers who died in the Battle of Princeton, 1777. Though the American troops lost one of their finest leaders, General William Mercer, in the fight, their stunning victory over the British under the leadership of General George Washington was an important triumph in the Revolutionary War.

During the Revolutionary War few American troops had a formal uniform. At Skylands, in Jockey Hollow, a modern-day "militiaman" demonstrates the informal dress of most colonial soldiers.

Aaron Burr and former U.S. Secretary of the Treasury Alexander Hamilton were long-time rivals. After a number of fierce political disputes, the two men decided to undertake a duel to the death. Burr, shown here in an engraving by Enoch G. Gridley, was the victor.

By the 1760s the colony had about 100,000 people, and there were rumblings of the coming Revolution. England had imposed severe taxes and restricted the trade of the colony, and the people were becoming discontented. The first Provincial Congress assembled in New Brunswick in 1774 and appointed delegates to the Continental Congress at Philadelphia. On July 2, 1776, the last royal governor of New Jersey was expelled, and the leaders of New Jersey adopted a combined state constitution and declaration of independence. As far as New Jersey was concerned, the Revolution was on.

From that time until the surrender of Lord Cornwallis at Yorktown in 1781, New Jersey knew no peace. The state became known as "the pathway of the Revolution," as the Americans and the British fought nearly 100 engagements on its soil. The most important of these battles were Trenton in 1776, Princeton in 1777, and Monmouth in 1778. Before the Battle of Trenton, George Washington made his famous surprise crossing of the Delaware River on Christmas night, and captured a garrison of Hessian mercenary troops who were in the employ of the British. Washington and his army crossed and recrossed New Jersey four times, shivering through two winters at Morristown and a third at Bound Brook. Tories—colonists loyal to the English Crown—took control of the southern Pine Barrens and waged guerrilla war from there. During the Revolutionary War, two New Jersey cities served temporarily as the national capital: Princeton, from June 30 to November 4, 1783, and Trenton, from November 1 to December 24, 1784.

New Jersey was the third state to ratify the Constitution, in 1787. William Livingston was appointed the first governor, and the state capital was established at Trenton in 1790. One of the most famous duels of all time was fought at Weehawken in 1804, when Aaron Burr, Vice-President of the United States, shot and killed his political rival, Alexander Hamilton. During the War of 1812, in which the United States again fought the British, it was a New Jersey man, Captain James Lawrence, who gave the United States Navy its motto: "Don't give up the ship!"

This engraving, completed two years after the famous Hamilton/Burr duel, depicts the exact spot in Weehawken where Hamilton fell.

During the early 1800s, New Jersey made major improvements in its transportation system, including new turnpikes, canals, and railroads. Better transportation in the state was important to the industrial growth that has continued to the present day.

In 1884 New Jersey became much more democratic when it adopted a new state constitution, which provided for a bill of rights and direct election of the governor by the people. The following year Charles C. Stratton became the first New Jersey governor elected by popular vote.

During the Civil War (1861–65), New Jersey seemed to be of two minds about the conflict. Some 88,000 men from the state served in the Union Army during the war, but many New Jersey residents were pro-South. Indeed, New Jersey was one of only three states in the Union that did not support the re-election of President Abraham Lincoln in 1864.

During the late 1800s, New Jersey, unlike most other states, allowed the formation of trusts, or business and industrial monopolies. This meant that many of the nation's powerful trusts made the state their home. The same thing was true for holding companies—firms that owned or controlled the stocks and policies of other companies. By the turn of the century, hundreds of these companies had been licensed to set up headquarters in New Jersey, which gave a big boost to the state's economy.

Industrial development was on the rise, too. New Jersey factories were busy turning out elevators, sewing machines, steam locomotives, and other up-to-the-minute products. The farming and food-processing industries expanded, also, as did the iron and steel factories. As a result, the population of New Jersey increased in the early years of the twentieth century. Thousands of immigrants began coming to the cities to work in factories: by 1910 about half the population of the Garden State had either been born outside the United States or had parents who had come from other countries. For the first time, more people lived in New Jersey cities than on New Jersey farms.

Thomas A. Edison (center) and several of his close assistants pose with an early phonograph outside their laboratory in West Orange, New Jersey, 1888. Edison called his West Orange laboratory the "invention factory."

In 1910 New Jersey elected as governor the progressive Woodrow Wilson, a former president of Princeton University, and state government began to change for the better. Laws were passed to provide direct primary elections, workman's compensation for job-related injuries or illness, and a public-utilities commission. Business monopolies were restricted. This forward-looking change in state government led to Wilson's election as President of the United States in 1912 and his re-election in 1916. He was a staunch advocate of world peace, who wore out his health seeking support for the League of Nations after World War I.

Fort Lee became the motion picture capital of the world in the early 1900s because of the pioneering film work being done in New Jersey by Thomas Alva Edison. Early stars such as Mary Pickford, Fatty Arbuckle, and Pearl White made many films in the state, which served as a "Wild West" location before the movie industry moved to Hollywood, California.

During World War I, Hoboken was a major port, and thousands of American servicemen left for France from that city on the Hudson River. Camp Dix and Camp Merrit were set up as huge military training centers, and New Jersey factories turned out vast quantities of chemicals, munitions, and ships to aid the war effort.

The years from 1900 to 1930 were years of expansion for the state. The population nearly doubled, and the value of products manufactured in New Jersey grew from $500 million to $4 billion. The state moved into its role as an electronics and chemical giant in the 1940s. New Jersey was a leader in the production of communications equipment, munitions, ships, and uniforms during World War II. Huge numbers of servicemen were trained at Camp Kilmer and Fort Dix.

During the 1950s, New Jersey's transportation system was expanded by construction of both the New Jersey Turnpike, which crosses the state diagonally from southwest to northeast, and the Garden State Parkway, which runs the length of New Jersey's east coast.

Today New Jersey is a state of large cities and small farms, with a wealth of scenic beauty and recreational facilities. New Jersey's cities contain vast industrial complexes, and its farms earn a larger gross income per acre than those of any other state.

As governor of New Jersey and later as president, Woodrow Wilson worked for many progressive programs.

The People

Ninety percent of New Jerseyans live in metropolitan areas. This percentage of city dwellers is the highest in the nation. Roughly 87 percent of New Jersey's residents were born in the United States. Of those born in other countries, the largest number came from Italy. Roman Catholics make up the state's largest religious body.

Famous People

Many famous people were born in the state of New Jersey. Here are a few:

Artists

Charles Addams 1912-1988, Westfield. Cartoonist for *The New Yorker*.

Asher Brown Durand 1796-1886, Jefferson Village. Painter, engraver, and illustrator; founder of the National Academy of Design

Alfred Stieglitz 1864-1946, Hoboken. Photographer: founder of the Photo-Secession Group—often called the "Father of Modern Photography"

Business Leaders

Juan Trippe 1899-1981, Sea Bright. Founder and president of Pan American World Airways

William H. Vanderbilt 1821-85, New Brunswick. President of the New York Central Railroad

Montgomery Ward 1843-1913, Chatham. Founder of the mail order house that bears his name

Entertainers

Bud Abbott 1895-1974, Asbury Park. Half of the Abbott and Costello comedy team

Lou Costello 1908-59, Paterson. Half of the Abbott and Costello comedy team

Michael Douglas b. 1944, New Brunswick. Movie producer, director, and Academy Award winning actor: *Wall Street*

John Forsythe b. 1918, Penns Grove. Movie and television actor: *Dynasty*.

Ernie Kovacs 1919-62, Trenton. Television and movie comedian

Jerry Lewis b. 1926, Newark. Television and movie comedian: *The Patsy, King of Comedy*

Ozzie Nelson 1906-75, Jersey City. Bandleader and television actor: *The Adventures of Ozzie and Harriet*

Jack Nicholson b. 1937, Neptune. Two-time Academy Award-winning actor: *One Flew Over the Cuckoo's Nest*

Eva Marie Saint b. 1924, Newark. Academy Award-winning movie actress: *On The Waterfront, Nothing in Common*

Loretta Swit b. 1943, Passaic. Movie and television actress: *M*A*S*H**

John Travolta b. 1954, Englewood. Television and movie actor: *Saturday Night Fever*

Explorers

Edwin E. "Buzz" Aldrin, Jr. b. 1930, Montclair. Astronaut: the second man to set foot on the moon

Zebulon Pike 1779-1813, Lumberton. Led expedition to explore the Louisiana Purchase, discovered Pike's Peak

Government Officials

William J. Brennan, Jr. b. 1906, Newark. Supreme Court justice

New Jersey's Bruce Springsteen is one of rock music's popular stars.

Aaron Burr 1756-1836, Newark. United States Vice-President under Jefferson

Grover Cleveland 1837-1908, Caldwell. Twenty-second and 24th President of the United States

Jonathan Dayton 1760-1824, Elizabeth. Youngest signer of the Constitution of the United States

Peter Rodino, Jr. b. 1909, Newark. Congressman: Chaired the Richard M. Nixon impeachment hearings

Military Figures

James Lawrence 1781-1813, Burlington. Naval captain in the War of 1812; his dying words were "Don't give up the ship "

Mary "Molly Pitcher" McCauley 1754-1832, Trenton. Revolutionary War heroine who carried water and fired cannon at the Battle of Monmouth

Daniel Morgan 1736-1802, Hunterdon County. Revolutionary War general who won the Battle of Cowpens

Scholars

Van Wyck Brooks 1886-1963, Plainfield. Pulitzer Prize-winning historian: *The Flowering of New England*

Astronaut Edwin "Buzz" Aldrin was the second man on the moon.

Nicholas Murray Butler 1862-1947, Elizabeth. Nobel Peace Prize-winning president of Columbia University

Alfred C. Kinsey 1894-1956, Hoboken. Zoologist and sexologist: *Sexual Behavior in the Human Male* and other studies

Joshua Lederberg b. 1925, Montclair. Nobel Prize-winning geneticist

Edmund Wilson 1895-1972, Red Bank. Literary critic: *To the Finland Station, Patriotic Gore*

Social Reformer

Alice Paul 1885-1977,

Moorestown. A leader of the woman-suffrage movement

Singers and Musicians
Count Basie 1904-84, Red Bank. Pianist, composer, and big band leader

Bette Midler b. 1945, Paterson. Singer and movie actress: *Ruthless People, Outrageous Fortune*

Paul Robeson 1898-1976, Princeton. Concert singer and actor

Frank Sinatra b. 1915, Hoboken. Singer and Academy Award-winning actor: *From Here to Eternity, The Manchurian Candidate*

Bruce Springsteen b. 1949, Freehold. Rock singer

Sarah Vaughan b. 1924, Newark. Jazz singer

Frederica von Stade b. 1945, Somerville. Operatic mezzo-soprano

Dionne Warwick b. 1941, East Orange. Pop singer

Sports Personalities
Rick Barry b. 1944, Elizabeth. Hall of Fame basketball player

Dick Button b. 1929, Englewood. Olympic gold medal figure skater and television sports broadcaster

Franco Harris b. 1950, Fort Dix. Football running back

Joe "Ducky" Medwick 1911-75, Carteret. Hall of Fame baseball outfielder

Johnny Vander Meer b. 1914, Prospect Park. The only professional baseball pitcher to throw two consecutive no-hitters, June 11 and 15, 1938

Jersey Joe Walcott b. 1914, Merchantville. Former world heavyweight boxing champion

Writers
Judy Blume b. 1938, Elizabeth. Novelist for young readers

James Fenimore Cooper 1789-1851, Burlington. Novelist: *The Last of the Mohicans* and other historical novels

Norman Cousins b. 1915, Union Hill. Author and editor

Stephen Crane 1871-1900, Newark. Novelist: *The Red Badge of Courage, The Open Boat and Other Tales*

Dorothy Gilman b. 1923, New Brunswick. Mystery writer: *The Amazing Mrs. Pollifax* and other mysteries

Joyce Kilmer 1886-1918, New Brunswick. Poet

Anne Morrow Lindbergh b. 1906, Englewood. Writer and poet: *Gift from the Sea, Bring Me a Unicorn,* and other works

Count Basie, the legendary band leader and jazz pianist.

Norman Mailer b. 1923, Long Branch. Novelist: *The Naked and the Dead , The Executioner's Song,* and other works

Mary O'Hara 1885-1980, Cape May Point. Novelist: *My Friend Flicka*

Dorothy Parker 1893-1967, West End. Reviewer and writer of short stories and verse: *After Such Pleasures*

Philip Roth b. 1933, Newark. Novelist: *Goodbye, Columbus , Portnoy's Complaint*

Edward Stratemeyer 1862-1930, Elizabeth. Novelist: creator of the Nancy Drew and Hardy Boys series, often used a pseudonym.

Albert Payson Terhune 1872-1942, Newark. Novelist: *Lad, A Dog*

William Carlos Williams 1883-1963, Rutherford. Poet: *Paterson, Pictures From Breughel*

Alexander Woollcott 1887-1943, Phalanx. Drama and literary critic

Colleges and Universities

Here are some of the many colleges and universities in New Jersey, with their locations, dates of founding, and enrollment.

Bloomfield College, Bloomfield, 1868, 2,036

Caldwell College, Caldwell, 1939, 1,339

College of Saint Elizabeth, Convent Station, 1899, 1,298

Drew University, Madison, 1866, 2,045

Fairleigh Dickinson University, Madison, 1958, 8,451

Georgian Court College, Lakewood, 1908, 2,503

Jersey City State College, Jersey City, 1927, 7,193

Montclair State College, Upper Monclair, 1908, 13,657

New Jersey Institute of Technology, Newark, 1881, 7,697

Princeton University, Princeton, 1746, 6,438

Rider College, Lawrenceville, 1865, 5,484

Ramapo College of New Jersey, Mahwah, 1969, 4,636

Rutgers, The State University of New Jersey, 48,572; *Camden College of Arts and Sciences*, 1927, 2,672; *College of Engineering*, New Brunswick, 1864, 2,454; *College of Nursing*, Newark, 1956, 391; *College of Pharmacy*, New Brunswick, 1927, 858; *Cook College*, New Brunswick, 1921, 2,908; *Douglass College*, New Brunswick, 1918, 3,181; *Livingston College*, New Brunswick, 1969, 3,645; *Mason Gross School of Arts*, New Brunswick, 1976, 630; *Newark College of Arts*

and Sciences, 1939, 3,782; *Rutgers College*, New Brunswick, 1766, 8,550; *University College Camden*, 1939, 851; *University College Newark*, 1934, 2,000; *University College New Brunswick*, 1934, 3,249

Seton Hall University, South Orange, 1856, 9,970

Stevens Institute of Technology, Hoboken, 1870, 3,240

Trenton State College, Trenton, 1855, 6,170

Upsala College, East Orange, 1893, 1,163

William Paterson College, Wayne, 1855, 9,391

Where To Get More Information

The State of New Jersey Division of Travel and Tourism
51 Commerce Street
Newark, NJ 06102
Or Call 1-800-JERSEY-7

New York

The great seal of New York was adopted in 1778. On it is pictured a figure of Justice and a figure of Liberty, with a crown at her feet to signify that kings have been rejected. A New York river scene is in the center, and an American eagle perches on a globe at the top.

CANADA

Plattsburgh

Burlington

LAKE ONTARIO

Watertown

Oswego

Rome

Lockport

Niagara Falls

Rochester

Syracuse

Utica

Gloversville

Amsterdam

Schenectad

Buffalo

West Seneca

Cooperstown

Albany ★

Troy

LAKE ERIE

NEW YORK

Ithaca

Hudson River

Jamestown

Olean

Elmira

Binghamton

Kingston

HYDE PARK ■

Poughkeepsie

Middletown

WEST POINT ■

PENNSYLVANIA

Newburgh

TARRYTOWN ■

NEW JERSEY

Yonkers

Lo

New York City

★ State Capital
● Cities or towns
■ OF SPECIAL INTEREST

| 0 | 10 | 20 | | 40 | | 60 | | 80 | | 100 | | 120 | | 140 | | 160 | | 180 | | 200 | | 220 | Miles |
| 0 | 10 | 20 | | 40 | | 60 | | 80 | | 100 | | 120 | | 140 | | 160 | 180 | | 200 | 220 | 240 | 260 | 280 | 300 | | 350 | Kilometres |

NEW YORK
At a Glance

VERMONT

ASSACHUSETTS

NNECTICUT

Island Sound

Capital: Albany

Major Industries: Communications, finance, timber, minerals, fishing, wine, fruits, vegetables, dairy products

State Flag

State Bird: Bluebird

State Flower: Rose
Nickname: The Empire State

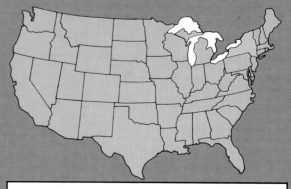

Size: 49,108 square miles (30th largest)
Population: 18,119,416 (2nd largest)

35

State Flag
   New York adopted its flag in 1901 and modified it in 1909. The background is blue and in the center is the state seal.

State Motto
Excelsior
   The Latin motto means "Ever Upward," and it was adopted in 1778 to indicate progress. It appeared on the first coat of arms of the state.

At Niagara Falls in upstate New York, on the border with Canada, 500,000 tons of water a minute plunge into the gorge at the bottom.

State Capital

Between 1777 and 1797, New York had a series of three capitals—Kingston, Poughkeepsie, and New York City. In 1797 Albany was made the capital.

State Name and Nicknames

In 1664 the English took over New Netherland from the Dutch, changing the name of both the city and the colony to New York. This was in honor of the Duke of York and Albany, the brother of England's king, Charles II.

New York State is most commonly nicknamed the *Empire State* because of its huge number of natural resources as well as its wealth. It is occasionally called the *Excelsior State* for its motto or the *Knickerbocker State* for the knee breeches worn by the early Dutch settlers.

State Flower

The rose (family Rosaceae) was adopted by the state legislature of New York in

The sugar maple is the state tree and a prime source of maple syrup.

1955, but no specific color has been designated.

State Tree

Adopted in 1956, the sugar maple, *Acer saccharum*, is the state tree of New York.

State Bird

The first state bird of New York was the robin, *Turdus migratorius*, but in the 1927-1928 legislative session, a vote was held indicating that the bluebird, *Sialia sialis*, was more popular with the state legislature. In 1970 the bluebird was

adopted as the official state bird.

State Animal

The American beaver, *Castor canadensis*, was adopted as the state animal in 1975 because of its economic importance in the early days of New York.

State Baked Good

The apple muffin was chosen as the state baked good in 1987.

State Fish

The brook or speckled trout, *Salvelinus fontinalis*, a delicious freshwater food fish, was adopted as the state fish in 1975.

State Fossil

Eurypterus remipes, an extinct relative of the king crab or sea scorpion, was adopted as the state fossil in 1984.

State Fruit

The apple, because of the many orchards in the state,

The beaver is the state animal.

was named the state fruit in 1976.

State Gem
  The garnet, mined in the Adirondack Mountains, was

New York's state fruit is the apple.

adopted in 1969.

State Insect
The ladybug, *Coccinella novemnotata,* was chosen as state insect in 1989.

State Song
  "I Love New York," words and music by Steve Karmen.

Population
  The population of New York in 1992 was 18,119,416, making it the second most populous state. There are 383.7 people per square mile.

Industries
  The principal industries of the state of New York are manufacturing, finance, communications, tourism, and transportation. The chief products are books and periodicals, clothing and apparel, pharmaceuticals, machinery, instruments, toys and sporting goods, electronic equipment, and automotive and aircraft components.

Agriculture
  The chief crops of the state are apples, cabbage, cauliflower, celery, cherries, grapes, corn, peas, snap beans, and sweet corn. Other agricultural products include milk, cheese, maple syrup, and wine. New York is also a livestock state, and there are estimated to be some 1.6 million cattle; 103,000 hogs and pigs; 92,000 sheep; and 9.8 million chickens, geese, turkeys, and ducks on its farms. Lumbering is important, and cement, crushed stone, sand, gravel, and salt are found here. Commercial fishing brings in some $53.2 million per year.

Government
  The govenor, the lieutenant governor, the attorney general, and the comptroller are all elected to four-year terms. The state legislature, which meets annually, consists of a 60-member senate and 150-member assembly, all of

A dairy farmer prepares a field in upstate New York.

whose members are elected by district. The most recent state constitution was adopted in 1894. In addition to its two U.S. senators, New York has 34 representatives in the U.S. House of Representatives. The state has 36 votes in the electoral college.

Sports

New York's colleges and secondary schools carry on a proud tradition in athletics. In 1954, Schenectady won the Little League World Series. Then another New York Little League team, Mid-Island of Staten Island, took the title in 1964. On the college level, City College of New York won the national basketball championship in 1950, and in football, Columbia won the Rose Bowl in 1934, and Fordham won the Sugar Bowl in 1942.

In professional sports, Buffalo has two major-league teams—the Bills of the National Football League play at Rich Stadium, and the Sabres of the National Hockey League play at the Buffalo Memorial Auditorium. In Hempstead, Long Island, the Islanders of the National Hockey League play at the Nassau Veterans Memorial Coliseum. New York City has a number of professional teams—the Mets of the National League play baseball at Shea Stadium, and the Yankees of the American League play baseball at Yankee Stadium. Madison Square Garden is the home of the Knicks of the National Basketball Association and the Rangers of the National Hockey League. The two professional football teams, the Jets and the Giants, are franchised in New York, but play at the New Jersey Meadowlands Complex.

Major Cities

Albany (population 100,031). Settled in 1624, Albany marks the spot where Henry Hudson ended his voyage up the Hudson River in 1609. Albany was founded by the Dutch, Norwegians, Danes, Germans, and Scots. Albany, earlier known as Fort Orange and Beverwyck, was renamed in 1664 in honor of the Duke of

York and Albany. It had become a thriving trade center by 1754. The capital of the state, it has long been a transportation center.

Things to see in Albany: The State Capitol, the Governor Nelson A. Rockefeller Empire State Plaza, the New York State Museum, the Shaker Heritage Society, the Albany Institute of History and Art, the Schuyler Mansion State Historic Site (1761), Arbor Hill (1798), Historic Cherry Hill (1787), and the Crailo State Historic Site (1710).

Buffalo (population 328,175). Settled in 1679, planned in 1803-04, and

The Albany skyline at night.

modeled after Washington, D.C., Buffalo was burned by the British during the War of 1812. A few months later its 500 citizens came back and rebuilt the town. The opening of the Erie Canal in 1825 made Buffalo the major transportation link between East and West and brought trade and prosperity to the region. The opening of the Saint Lawrence Seaway in 1959 solidified the city's position as a transportation center.

Things to see in Buffalo: The City Hall Observation Tower, the Guaranty Building, the residences built by Frank Lloyd Wright, the Theodore Roosevelt Inaugural National Historic Site, the Albright-Knox Art Gallery, the Buffalo and Erie County Historical Society, the Buffalo Museum of Science, Allentown, the Buffalo Zoological Gardens, the Buffalo and Erie County Naval and Servicemen's Park, the Buffalo and Erie County Botanical Gardens, and the Darien Lake Theme Park.

New York City (population 7,322,564). What is now called Manhattan was first settled in 1615 as a trading post for the Dutch West India Company. In 1626 Peter Minuit bought the island from the Indians and named it New Amsterdam. The name was changed to New York in 1664 when the English took over. New York was occupied by the British from 1776 until the end of the Revolutionary War when it became the first capital of the United States. In 1898 New York merged with Brooklyn, the Bronx, Queens, and Staten Island. Today it is the most populous city in the country and can lay claim to being a world leader in finance, business, communications, and culture.

Things to see in Manhattan : The Statue of Liberty National Monument, Ellis Island, Castle Clinton National Monument, Bowling Green, the United States Custom House

(1907), Fraunces Tavern museum, Trinity Church (1846), Wall Street (with both the New York Stock Exchange and the American Stock Exchange), Federal Hall National Memorial (1842), the Chase

The Statue of Liberty stands on Liberty Island in the midst of New York's busy harbor.

Manhattan Bank, the Federal Reserve Bank of New York, the World Trade Center, Saint Paul's Chapel, the Woolworth Building, City Hall Park, the Brooklyn Bridge, Chinatown, SoHo, Greenwich Village, Washington Square, the Church of the Ascension (1841), the Public Theater, the garment district, the New York City Post Office, the Jacob K. Javits Convention Center, Madison Square Garden, the Empire State Building, the New York Public Library, the Schomburg Center for Research in Black Culture, the Chrysler Building, the United Nations, Times Square and the theater district, Rockefeller Center, Saint Patrick's Cathedral, City Center Theater, Temple Emanu-El, Central Park, Lincoln Center for the Performing Arts, the Cathedral Church of Saint John the Divine, the General Grant National Memorial, the Metropolitan Museum of Art, The Cloisters, The Solomon R. Guggenheim Museum, the Frick Collection, the Museum of Modern Art,

the Asia Society Galleries, the Whitney Museum of American Art, the Cooper-Hewitt Museum, the Grand Central Art Galleries, the Museum of Holography, the Studio Museum in Harlem, the International Center for Photography, El Museo del Barrio, the New York Historical Society, the Ukrainian Museum, the Jewish Museum, the Museum of the City of New York, the Washington Heights Museum Group, the Pierpont Morgan Library, the Theodore Roosevelt Birthplace National Historic Site, Bible House, the Hamilton Grange National Memorial, Dyckman House Park and Museum (1783), the Morris-Jumel Mansion (1765), the American Museum of Natural History, the Hayden Planetarium, the Astro Minerals Gallery of Gems, the Museum of Broadcasting, the Police Academy Museum, the Guinness Book of World Records Exhibit Hall, the South Street Seaport Museum, and the Museum of the American Indian.

Places to visit in the Bronx :
The Bronx Zoo, the New

The World Trade Center's twin towers rise high above the Manhattan skyline at the southern tip of the island. They are the second-tallest buildings in the world.

The United Nations building, located in midtown Manhattan, is a meeting place for leaders and diplomats from countries all over the world.

The Verrazano-Narrows Bridge links Brooklyn and Staten Island.

York Botanical Gardens, the Bronx Museum of the Arts, the Hall of Fame of Great Americans, the Van Cortlandt Mansion (1748), the Museum of Bronx History, the Edgar Allan Poe Cottage, the Bartow-Pell Mansion museum and gardens, Wave Hill, and City Island.

Places to visit in Brooklyn :
Brooklyn Heights, the Brooklyn Academy of Music, Prospect Park, the Brooklyn Botanic Gardens, the Brooklyn Museum, the Brooklyn Children's Museum, the Brooklyn Historical Society, Coney Island, Astroland Amusement Park, and the New York Aquarium.

Places to visit in Queens:
The John F. Kennedy International Airport, La Guardia Airport, Bowne House (1661), Flushing Meadows-Corona Park, the Isamu Noguchi studio and Museum, the Queens Museum, the New York Hall of Science, and the Queens Botanical Garden.

Places to visit on Staten Island :
The Staten Island Ferry, the Verrazano-Narrows Bridge, the Staten Island Museum, Snug Harbor Cultural Center, the Staten Island Children's Museum, the Staten Island Zoo, the Jacques Marchals Center of Tibetan Art, the High Rock Park Conservation Center, the Richmondtown Restoration, and the Conference House.

Rochester (population 230,356). Settled in 1803, the city soon became a major industrial and cultural center. It is located on the Genesee River in the midst of rich fruit-producing and truck-gardening country.
Places to visit in Rochester :
The International Museum of Photography at George Eastman House, the Rochester Museum and Science Center, the Strasenburgh Planetarium, the Margaret Woodbury Strong Museum, the Susan B. Anthony House, the

Rochester's Museum and Science Center includes the Strasenburgh Planetarium.

Campbell-Whittlesey House (1835), the Stone-Tolan House (1792), the Rochester Historical Society, the Memorial Art Gallery of the University of Rochester, Seneca Park and Zoo, the Victorian Doll Museum, and the Genesee Country Village Museum.

Syracuse (population 163,860). Settled in 1789 as a trading post, Syracuse was also a salt-producing town until 1900. Its industry began in 1793, when wooden plows were produced. Early in the 1800s a blast furnace was built to produce iron utensils and shot for the Army. The opening of the Erie Canal ensured the industrial future of Syracuse.

> *Places to visit in Syracuse :*
> The Onondaga Historical Association Museum, the Everson Museum of Art, Fort Sainte Marie de Gannentaha, the Salt Museum, the Daniel Parrish Witter Agricultural Museum, the Erie Canal Museum, Discovery Center, and the Beaver Lake Nature Center.

Places To Visit

The National Park Service maintains 13 areas in the state of New York: Fire Island National Seashore, Saratoga National Historical Park, Roosevelt-Vanderbilt National Historic sites, Sagamore Hill National Historic Site, Theodore Roosevelt Inaugural National Historic Site, Fort Stanwix National Monument, Theodore Roosevelt Birthplace Historic Site, The Statue of Liberty National Monument, Castle Clinton National Monument, Gateway National Recreation Area, Grant's Tomb National Memorial, Hamilton Grange National Memorial, and Federal Hall National Memorial. In addition, there are 85 state recreation areas.

Amsterdam: Fort Johnson. Built in 1749, it was the home of Sir William Johnson, the English superintendent of Indian affairs.

Arcade: Arcade and Attica Railroad. It offers a steam train ride through scenic countryside.

Auburn: Seward House. Built in 1816-17, this was the home of William Henry Seward, Lincoln's Secretary of State, who was a leading figure in the purchase of Alaska.

Bay Shore, Long Island: Sagtikos Manor. This house, built in 1692, was General Henry Clinton's headquarters during the Revolution.

Bethpage, Long Island: Old Bethpage Village Restoration. A working farm and 30 pre–Civil War buildings are located here.

Boonville: Constable Hall. Built around 1819, Constable Hall is a limestone Georgian mansion.

Canandaigua: Granger Homestead and Carriage Museum. Built in 1816, this was the home of Gideon Granger, postmaster general under Presidents Jefferson and Madison.

Canton: Silas Wright House and Museum. This Greek Revival house, built between 1832 and 1844, was the house of the lawyer and politician who was New York's governor from 1845 to 1847.

Catskill: Catskill Game Farm. A hands-on zoo, it contains deer, antelope, llamas, and other animals.

Cooperstown: National Baseball Hall of Fame and Museum. This building contains the Hall of Fame Gallery and a museum with displays on baseball's greatest moments.

Corning: Corning Glass Center. This center includes the Museum of Glass and the Steuben Glass Factory.

Cortland: 1890 House Museum. This opulent Victorian mansion of 30 rooms features fine woodwork, elaborate stenciling, and stained glass.

Coxsackie: Bronck Museum. One of the houses in this complex dates from 1663.

East Aurora: Millard Fillmore Museum. Built around 1825, this was the house that the 13th President erected for his wife.

East Hampton, Long Island: "Home Sweet Home" House and Windmill. This house, built in 1804, was the childhood home of John Howard Payne, who wrote the song "Home Sweet Home."

Fishkill: Mount Gulian. Built between 1730 and 1740, this was the headquarters of Baron von Steuben during the Revolutionary War and the birthplace of the Order of the Society of Cincinnati, the first veterans organization.

Garrison: Boscobel. Boscobel

The Corning Glass Center houses a museum and a glass factory.

is a beautifully restored mansion built in 1806 in the New York Federal style.

Howe Cave: Howe Caverns. Here is a series of caverns ranging from 160 to 200 feet below the surface, with an underground river and lake.

Hudson: Olana State Historic Site. This is the hilltop estate of Frederick Edwin Church, famous landscape painter of the Hudson River School. Built between 1870 and 1874, it offers spectacular views of the Hudson River and the Catskill Mountains.

Huntington, Long Island: Walt Whitman Birthplace State Historic Site. This boyhood home of the poet has been restored.

Hyde Park: Franklin D. Roosevelt National Historic Site. This was the family home of the 32d President, and the house dates from 1826. The F.D.R. presidential library is also here.

Kingston: Senate House State Historic Site. This is a simple stone residence dating from 1676 where the first New York State Senate met in 1777.

Lake George Village: Fort William Henry Museum.

Here is the 1755 fort, rebuilt from the original plans.

Lake Placid: John Brown Farm State Historic Site. This was the last home of the noted abolitionist.

Monroe: Museum Village in Orange County. Here are 33 buildings showing the crafts and technology of the 19th century.

Newburgh: Washington's Headquarters State Historic Site. This is the Jonathan Hasbrouck house (1750) that was Washington's headquarters for 16 1/2

months at the end of the Revolution.

New Paltz: Huguenot Street Old Stone Houses. Here are six stone houses (one dating from 1692).

Niagara Falls: Niagara Reservation State Park. This area features fine views of the falls as well as a geological museum.

Oyster Bay, Long Island: Sagamore Hill National Historic Site. From 1901 to 1909, this was President Theodore Roosevelt's summer White House.

Visitors to the Cave of the Winds at Niagara Falls.

Palmyra: Joseph Smith Home. Smith, founder of the Church of Jesus Christ of the Latter Day Saints (the Mormons), lived here as a young man.

Poughkeepsie: Locust Grove. Here is the house dating from 1830 where Samuel F.B. Morse, inventor of the telegraph, lived.

Rhinebeck: Old Rhinebeck Aerodrome. At Rhinebeck there is a collection of antique airplanes from 1908-37, some of which are still flown in air shows here.

Rome: Fort Stanwix National Monument. This is a restored earth-and-log fort on the original location of the 1758 fort.

Schenectady: Canal Square. This is a large block of shops in restored historic buildings.

Schuylerville: Saratoga National Historic Park. General Philip Schuyler House, dating from 1777, was the home of Schuyler, who fought Burgoyne in the Revolution.

Seneca Falls: National Women's Hall of Fame. Seneca Falls is known as the birthplace of the women's rights movement, and the hall honors

Boats tour Lake Placid in the summer months.

American women of distinction.

Southampton, Long Island: Old Halsey Homestead. This is one of the oldest English frame houses in the state and dates from 1648.

Tarrytown: Sunnyside. Built from 1835 to 1859, this was the home of writer Washington Irving.

Ticonderoga: Fort Ticonderoga. A restoration based on the original French plans, this fortification was built before the Revolution and changed hands repeatedly between 1757 and 1777.

West Point: The United States Military Academy. Before the academy was founded

in 1802, West Point was an active fort guarding the Hudson River.

Yonkers: Sherwood House. This is a restored colonial farm house.

Events

There are many events and organizations that schedule seasonal activities of various kinds in the state of New York. Here are some of them.

Sports: General Clinton Canoe Regatta (Bainbridge); harness racing at Batavia Downs (Batavia); Balloon Rally (Binghamton); B.C. Open PGA Golf Tournament

Horse racing at Saratoga Springs.

(Binghamton); harness racing at Buffalo Raceway (Buffalo); Horse racing at Finger Lakes Race Track (Canandaigua); Rushton Canoe Races (Canton); Antique Boat Show (Clayton); Model Boat Show Regatta (Clayton); Hall of Fame Baseball Game (Cooperstown); Soaring Contests (Elmira); Great Canoe Races (Freeport); National Trout Derby (Geneva); Winter Carnival (Gloversville); Horse racing at Goshen Historic Track (Goshen); On the Water Boat Show (Ithaca); Winter Carnival (Lake George Village); Rodeos (Lake Luzerne); Antique Classic Car Show (Malone); harness racing at Monticello Raceway (Monticello); New York City Marathon (New York); Whitewater Derby (North Creek); harness racing at Vernon Downs (Oneida); United States Open Tennis (Queens); horse racing at Belmont Park (Queens); horse racing at Aqueduct (Queens); World Series of Bocce (Rome); Alpo International Sled Dog Races (Saranac Lake); Winter Carnival (Saranac Lake); Willard Hammer Guideboat, Canoe, and War Canoe Races (Saranac Lake); Adirondack Canoe Classic (Saranac Lake); horse racing at Saratoga Race Track (Saratoga Springs); Saratoga Harness Racing (Saratoga Springs); OTB Grand Prix Tennis Tournament (Schenectady); Sailing Regatta (Schroon Lake); Polo Matches (Skaneateles); Eastern Snowmobile Race Association Races (Speculator); Intercollegiate Rowing Regatta (Syracuse); Incredible Journey Triathlon (Syracuse); Unlimited Hydroplane Regatta (Syracuse); Scottish Games (Syracuse); Ticonderoga Memorial Scottish Gathering (Ticonderoga); Fort Ticonderoga Muzzle Loading Rifle Shoot (Ticonderoga); Flatwater Weekend (Tupper Lake); Woodsmen's Days (Tupper Lake); Tinman Triathlon (Tupper Lake); U.S.-Canadian International Swim Meet (Watertown); Lumberjack Festival (Watertown); Watkins Glen International Race Circuit (Watkins Glen); International Road Racing (Watkins Glen); Inner Tube Regatta (Wellsville);

horse racing at Roosevelt Raceway (Westbury); Yonkers Marathon (Yonkers); harness racing at Yonkers Raceway (Yonkers).

Arts and Crafts: Tulip Festival (Albany); Arts/Crafts Fairs (Bolton Landing); Quality Antique Show in the Big Top (Bolton Landing); Duck, Decoy, and Wildlife Art Show (Clayton); Central New York Antiques Show and Sale (Cortland); Finger Lakes Antique Show (Ithaca); North Country Heritage Festival (Massena); Craft Days (Oneida); Lilac Time Festival (Rochester); Spirit of 17th-Century France (Syracuse); Autumn Crafts and Tasks Festival (Tarrytown); Antiques Fair (White Plains); Woodstock Artists Association Gallery (Woodstock).

Music: Carillon Concerts (Alfred); Binghamton Symphony (Binghamton); Tri-Cities Opera (Binghamton); B.C. Pops on the River (Binghamton); Summer Arts Festival (Brockport); Artfest (Buffalo); Buffalo Philharmonic (Buffalo); Brooklyn Academy of Music (Brooklyn); Brooklyn Philharmonic (Brooklyn); Finger Lakes Music Festival (Canandaigua); Chautauqua Symphony (Chautauqua);

Fiddlers' Fling (Clayton); Glimmerglass Opera (Cooperstown); Cooperstown Concert Series (Cooperstown); Smith Opera House (Geneva); Lake George Opera Festival (Glens Falls); Hunter County Music Festival (Hunter); National Polka Festival (Hunter); International Celtic Festival (Hunter); Summer Arts Festival (Huntington); Concerts by the Lake (Ithaca); Jones Beach Theatre (Jones Beach State Park); Lake Placid Center for the Arts (Lake Placid); American Wind Symphony Concerts (Medina); Caramoor Center for Music and the Arts (Mount Kisco); American

Symphony (New York); Carnegie Hall (New York); Central Park Concerts (New York); JVC Jazz Festival (New York); Little Orchestra Society of New York (New York); Metropolitan Opera (New York); New York City Opera (New York); New York Philharmonic (New York); Opera Orchestra of New York (New York); Philharmonia Virtuosi (New York); Niagara Summer Experience (Niagara Falls); International Seaway Festival (Ogdensburg); Hudson Valley Philharmonic (Poughkeepsie); Queens Symphony (Queens); Rochester Philharmonic (Rochester);

A concert at the Saratoga Performing Arts Center.

Saratoga Performing Arts Center (Saratoga Springs); Open-Air Concerts (Syracuse); Syracuse Opera (Syracuse); Syracuse Symphony (Syracuse); Summer Music on the Hudson Festival (Tarrytown); Westbury Music Fair (Westbury); Maverick Concerts (Woodstock).

Entertainment: Balloon Rally (Binghamton); Oneida County Fair (Boonville); Erie County Fair (Buffalo); Autumn Harvest Festival (Cooperstown); Chautauqua County Fair (Dunkirk); Toy Festival (East Aurora); Chemung County Fair (Elmira); Annual Return of the Sacandaga Swifts (Gloversville); Gouverneur and Saint Lawrence County Fair (Gouverneur); Panama Folk Festival (Jamestown); Lions Club Strawberry Festival and County Fair (Mattituck); Orange County Fair (Middletown); Ulster County Fair (New Paltz); Spring and Fall Festivals (New Rochelle); Chinese New Year (New York); Washington's Birthday Parade (New York); Saint Patrick's Day Parade (New York); Harbor Festival (New York); San Gennaro Festival (New York); Columbus Day Parade (New York); Hispanic Day Parade (New York); Thanksgiving Day Parade (New York); Fantasy

Island (Niagara Falls); Intertribal Pow-Wow (Niagara Falls); Festival of Lights (Niagara Falls); Tioga County Fair (Oswego); The Hill Cumorah Pageant (Palmyra); Dutchess County Fair (Rhinebeck); Riverhead County Fair (Riverhead); Monroe County Fair (Rochester); Allegany Indian Fair (Salamanca); Seneca Indian Fall Festival (Salamanca); Annual Air Show (Schenectady); Convention Days Celebration (Seneca Falls); Powwow (Southhampton); Balloon Festival (Syracuse); New York State Fair (Syracuse); Golden Harvest Festival (Syracuse); World's Largest Garage Sale and Foliage Festival (Warrensburg); New York Renaissance Festival (Warwick); Irish Festival (Watertown); Jefferson County Fair (Watertown); The Great Wellsville Balloon Rally (Wellsville).

Tours: Stone House Day (Kingston); Walkabout (Schenectady); Candlelight Tours (Tarrytown).

Theater: Cider Mill Playhouse (Binghamton); Studio Arena Theatre (Buffalo); Shea's Buffalo Theater (Buffalo); Chautauqua Conservatory Theater (Chautauqua); Acting

Company (Chautauqua); Corning Summer Theater (Corning); Cortland Repertory Theatre (Cortland); John Drew Theater at Guild Hall (East Hampton); Mark Twain Drama at the Domes (Elmira); Hangar Theatre Company (Ithaca); Ulster Performing Arts Center (Kingston); SUNY College Summer Repertory Theatre (New Paltz); New York Shakespeare Festival (New York); Broadway and Off-Broadway theaters (New York); Eastman Theater (Rochester); GeVa Theatre (Rochester); Proctor's Theatre (Schenectady); Landmark Theatre (Syracuse); Syracuse Stage (Syracuse).

New York is host to numerous fairs and festivals.

Montauk Point, on the tip of Long Island.

Along the banks of the Hudson River.

Although much of the Adirondack range is mountainous, it does contain areas that are suitable for farming.

The Land and the Climate

New York is the only state with borders on the Atlantic Ocean and the Great Lakes. It has a 127-mile Atlantic coastline and 371 miles of shoreline on Lake Ontario and Lake Erie. Its tallest mountains are in the Adirondack range, in the northeastern part of the state, and the highest point in these mountains is Mount Marcy, at 5,344 feet. Waterways are important to the state's transportation system. The Hudson and the Mohawk are the chief rivers, followed by the Genesee and the Oswego. New York also has more than 8,000 lakes.

The Ice Age ended about 10,000 years ago, but during that time huge glaciers covered almost all of what is now New York State. Most of the soil here was deposited by these massive ice formations as they scattered stones, pebbles, and other materials over the surface of the land.

New York has seven major land regions. The Atlantic Coastal Plain takes in Long Island and Staten Island as part of the almost level plain stretching along the Atlantic Coast from Massachusetts to the tip of Florida. Broad sandy beaches can be found on the southern shore of Long Island. Fishing and recreation are an important source of income in this area.

The New England Upland, with its hills and low mountains, forms a narrow strip along the state's eastern edge, running from the south toward the northern border. In this area are the Taconic Mountains and the southern part of the Hudson River Valley.

The many ports of Long Island are home to thousands of pleasure boats and other craft like this one in Greenport.

Much of New York State is still naturally wild. Ausable Chasm is a good example of the heavily wooded, rocky land common to the Adirondack region.

The Hudson-Mohawk Lowland covers most of the remaining Hudson River Valley and the whole of the Mohawk River Valley. This strip west of the New England Upland is from 10 to 30 miles wide. It is the only large break in the Appalachian Mountains, and cuts through highlands that can reach heights of a thousand feet or more. This has made it a major "roadway" for trade since Indian times. The plains in this area support countless farms, orchards, and dairies, and the many waterfalls here serve as a source of hydroelectric power.

The Adirondack Upland is in the northeastern part of New York— a circular area whose mountains are perhaps the oldest in North America. These uplands are wild and beautiful, with their mountains, lakes, streams, and waterfalls. The soil here cannot support much farming, but there are lumber mills and iron ore mines.

A view of Rochester, one of the biggest cities in western New York.

The Catskill countryside is dotted with many covered bridges like this one.

Along the south bank of the St. Lawrence River lies the St. Lawrence Lowland, bordering the Adirondack Upland to the north. Only about 20 miles wide, this region of rolling hills contains many dairy farms and apple orchards, and the tourist industry is important to the Thousand Islands of the St. Lawrence River.

The Erie-Ontario Lowland lies south of the two Great Lakes for which it is named; part of it was once the bottom of an ancient glacial lake. In other parts of the Lowland, moraines, or glacial deposits, form another region of rolling hills. Southeast of Rochester are many drumlins—oval-shaped hills from 50 to 300 feet high. These, too, were formed by the old glaciers. The region has some of the most productive soil in the state, and there are many fruit and truck farms here, as well as dairy farms and plant nurseries.

The Appalachian Plateau covers most of southern New York State, lying south and west of the Hudson-Mohawk Lowland and south of the Erie-Ontario Lowland. In this area, glaciers and rivers have formed hills and valleys in the Finger Lakes area and mountains in the Catskills. Dairy farms are common in this region, as are vineyards, nurseries, and truck farms. It is a scenic area that is popular with vacationers.

The climate of New York State varies greatly from region to region because of the vast differences in altitude and exposure to bodies of water. The coastal areas have the hottest summers, mildest winters, and least snow. The Adirondack Highlands have the heaviest snows, the coldest winters, and the coolest summers. The average temperatures along the coastal plain are 32 degrees F. in January and 76 degrees F. in July. The Adirondacks average 18 degrees F. in January and 64 degrees F. in July. Precipitation here varies between 32 and 45 inches per year, including melted snow.

Above:
New York is one of the country's leading producers of still and sparkling wine. Large vineyards, like this one in Naples, are common sights in the southern half of the state.

Top left:
A view of Lake Ontario, which borders New York at the northwestern part of the state.

The History

A harvest mask made by the Onondaga Indians. The Onondaga are one of the Five Nations of the Iroquois and are native to New York.

Before the arrival of the Europeans, there were two Indian groups in what would become New York State. One group was the Algonkian family, which was subdivided into the Delaware, Mohican, Montauk, Munsee, and Wappinger tribes. The other group was the Iroquois, who made up the Five Nations: the Cayuga, Mohawk, Oneida, Onondaga, and Seneca tribes. The Indians farmed, fished, and hunted.

Giovanni da Verrazano, an Italian who was hired by King Francis I of France to explore northern North America, sailed into New York Bay in 1524, and he may have discovered the Hudson River. But no one established strong territorial claims until Henry Hudson piloted the *Half Moon* up the river that bears his name in 1609. The Dutch, for whom he was sailing, founded trading posts at New Amsterdam and at Fort Nassau, 150 miles north. Hudson was looking for a Northwest Passage to the Orient, but his voyage gave the Netherlands a claim to the territory comprising much of present-day New York. In that same year, the French explorer Samuel de Champlain entered the northern part of New York from Quebec. This gave the French a claim to part of the land.

Having built up a profitable fur trade with the Indians of the Hudson Valley, the Dutch merchants formed the Dutch West India Company in 1621, and the government of the Netherlands gave the company the right to trade in what was then called New Netherland for the next 24 years. In 1624 settlement began in earnest with some 30 families sent by the company to the New World. Some of these families founded Fort Orange, the first permanent white settlement in the colony. The next year a group of Dutch colonists built a fort and laid out a town on Manhattan Island—now the heart of New York City—naming the community New Amsterdam. In 1626 the Dutch governor, Peter Minuit, bought Manhattan from the Indians for goods worth 60 Dutch guilders (about $24).

A depiction by John Simon of Etow Oh Koam, an Iroquois chief. The portrait is entitled "King of the River Nation."

This 1642 engraving shows some of New York's original Dutch settlers in their new homeland. Their settlement was called "New Amsterdam."

During the next few years, several towns were established by the Dutch—Wiltwyck, Rensselaerswyck, Breuckelen, Schenectady, and others. Meanwhile, many English settlers from Connecticut and Massachusetts had moved into Long Island. For a time they cooperated with the Dutch, but King Charles II of England coveted the region, and he gave his brother James, the Duke of York, a charter for the territory of New Netherland. In 1664 a British fleet dropped anchor in the harbor of New Amsterdam, and Peter Stuyvesant, the Dutch governor, surrendered without a fight in a bloodless coup—a sudden takeover. Names changed all over the territory. New Amsterdam became New York, as did New Netherland. Fort Orange became Albany; Wiltwyck became Kingston; Rensselaerswyck became Rensselaer; Breuckelen became Brooklyn.

For some time the colony prospered under English rule. Then the French, who had claimed the Lake Champlain area in the north and named it New France, began to take a real interest in the territory. In 1669 the French explorer Robert Cavelier, Sieur de la Salle, entered the Niagara region. Then, in 1689, war broke out in Europe between England and France, and New York became a battleground—an extension of that war. The French built a fortress at Crown Point on Lake Champlain in 1731. They began a steady harassment from the north, sometimes alone and sometimes with Indian allies. Battles were fought at Crown Point, at Niagara, at Fort Ticonderoga, and in many other places, with the Algonkians helping the French and the Iroquois siding with the English and the Loyalists. But despite the loss of life among settlers in what came to be called the French and Indian Wars, the colony continued to prosper. The warring countries finally signed a peace treaty—the Treaty of Paris—in 1763, and France lost most of her New World holdings.

A modern-day example at Fort Ticonderoga of what soldiers looked like during the Colonial War.

Some traces of the Dutch settlers can still be found today. In Tarrytown, New York, this old church is a well-preserved example of Dutch design and craftsmanship.

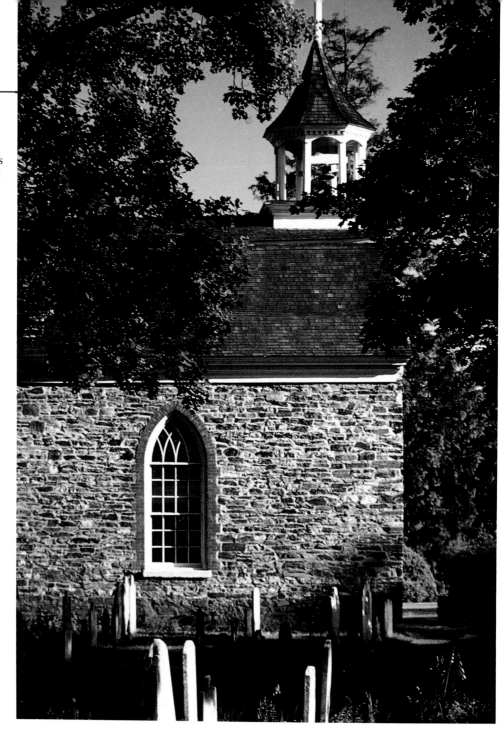

A souvenir from 1850 that shows what New York City looked like at that time.

The British colonists in New York had been granted a Charter of Liberties and Privileges in 1683: it guaranteed a representative assembly with control over taxation, but this began to erode during the reign of King George II. An important victory for freedom of speech and of the press was won in 1735, when the publisher of the *New York Weekly Journal,* John Peter Zenger, who had criticized the English governor, was found not guilty of libel.

It was at Albany in 1754 that the first Colonial Congress adopted a Plan of Union incorporating human-rights principles. This was the initial step toward uniting the 13 original colonies. Many New Yorkers did not like the presence of British troops, the authority of royal judges, or the taxes levied by the British Parliament. Others—the Loyalists or Tories—upheld the British Government and refused to call themselves American patriots.

New York's strategic location made it the place in which a third of the battles of the Revolutionary War were fought—on land and in the water. American patriots won two of the major New York battles. The first was the Battle of Oriskany in August 1777; even more important was the Battle of Saratoga in October 1777, in which British General Burgoyne's defeat turned the tide of the war in the colonists' favor.

On July 9, 1776, the Provincial Congress of New York, meeting in White Plains, approved the Declaration of Independence that the Continental Congress had adopted on July 4. The following year New

York adopted a state constitution with three basic branches of government—legislative, executive, and judicial—12 full years before the Federal Government worked out this form for its own use. George Clinton was installed as the first governor of the state.

When New York ratified the United States Constitution, it became the 11th state to enter the union. No one knows how many New York colonists were loyal to the British cause, but after the Revolution, 30,000 persons left the state. New York City served as the capital of the United States from 1785 to 1790. George Washington was inaugurated the nation's first president in 1789 in New York's Federal Hall.

After the Revolution, settlement of New York State progressed rapidly at the expense of the native peoples. Washington had sent an expedition to subdue the Iroquois in 1779, and troops led by General James Clinton raided Indian villages throughout the Mohawk Valley. These soldiers joined others commanded by General John Sullivan and marched through the Finger Lakes region to the Genesee Valley in Pennsylvania. The Iroquois were dispossessed and defeated, and many Revolutionary War veterans moved into the desirable territory.

During the War of 1812, much of the fighting took place in frontier regions near the New York-Canadian border. The joint land-lake victory of General Macomb and Commodore Macdonough at Plattsburg broke the strength of British attacks from the north. After the war, pioneers began to settle in the northern and western sections of the state, and by 1820 New York had reached a population level of over 1,370,000—greater than that of any other state.

New York's long-awaited Erie Canal opened in 1825, under the leadership of Governor DeWitt Clinton, the nephew of George Clinton: it provided low-cost transportation from the Great Lakes to the Atlantic. New industries sprang up from New York City to Buffalo, where the canal began. The development of railroads across the state soon followed.

Long before the beginning of the Civil War in 1861, most New Yorkers opposed slavery, but there were dissenters. In July of 1863 mobs rioted in New York City for four days in opposition to drafting men into the Union Army. The mobs set fires, looted, and killed or wounded about 1000 people. The riots were finally stopped by troops called in from the battlefields. Despite all this, New York provided more soldiers, supplies and money for the Union war effort than any other state.

After the Civil War, manufacturing increased all over New York, which had already become known as the Empire State. Waves of immigrants poured in to work in the factories, many of them from Italy, Poland, Russia, and other southern and eastern European countries. By 1900 there were more than 7,000,000 people living in the state. It led the nation in industry, finance, culture, and international trade. Millions of immigrants entered the country at New York City's Ellis Island, passing the great Statue of Liberty as they arrived.

Buffalo hosted a Pan American Exposition in 1901—an international fair that sought to promote understanding between North and South America. The governor of New York from 1899 to 1901 was Theodore Roosevelt, who came from a wealthy old family and had been the Commissioner of Police in New York City. He was a reformer, especially in the field of labor. Roosevelt became Vice-President of the United States under William McKinley. On September 6, 1901, just six months after his inauguration, McKinley was shot by an assassin at the opening ceremonies of the Exposition. Roosevelt became president eight days later when McKinley died.

When the United States entered World War I in 1917, New York City served as the main port from which troop ships sailed to and from Europe. During the Depression of the 1930s, Franklin Delano Roosevelt, a former governor of New York and a cousin of Theodore Roosevelt, became president of the United States. He served from 1933 until his death in 1945—the only U.S. President to be elected to a fourth term. His great popularity was a result of his aggressive leadership through the Depression and war years.

Another great World's Fair was held in New York in 1939 and 1940—this time in New York City. It celebrated "The World of

Niagara Falls, located in the westernmost region of New York State, is a natural wonder that has attracted visitors since the early nineteenth century.

Tomorrow" and introduced a working television set to the American public. Then came World War II, from 1941 to 1945, for which New York produced more war materials than any other state. Binghamton, Buffalo, New York City, Schenectady and other industrial cities converted their plants into war goods production centers that supplied the armed forces. New York Harbor was filled with troop ships again, and plane spotters manned the city's roofs.

The year after the war ended, the United Nations chose New York City as its headquarters. The peacekeeping organization moved into its new office complex on the East River in 1952, making New York a true world capital.

The St. Lawrence Seaway was opened in 1959, on the great river between New York State and the Canadian province of Ontario. Now New York's northern river and Great Lakes ports were ocean ports, with access to the Atlantic. Completion of the 559-mile New York State Thruway (later named for former Governor Thomas E. Dewey) made the state an even more important transportation center by 1960. Creation of the vast State University of New York made higher education available to more young men and women, and cooperation with Canada resulted in great hydroelectric projects along the St. Lawrence River and at Niagara Falls. Today the state of New York is one of the most progressive and productive in the nation.

New York City typifies the "melting pot," with its varied mix of people.

The People

About 85 percent of the residents of New York State live in metropolitan areas. New York City is the most populous city in the country. Both state and city have been called a "melting pot," where people of various races and countries have settled and adopted a common culture. Almost one in every seven people in the state was born in another country. One fourth of those who were born in the United States have a parent or parents who were born in another country. The largest groups of immigrants came from Italy, Germany, Russia, Poland, Ireland, Canada, Austria, and Great Britain.

The largest single religious body in the state is the Roman Catholic Church. New York has more Roman Catholics and more Jews than any other state.

Famous People

Many famous people were born in the state of New York. Here are a few:

Writers

James Baldwin 1924-87, NYC. Novelist: *Go Tell It on the Mountain, The Fire Next Time*

L. Frank Baum 1856-1919, Chittenango. Children's author: *The Wonderful Wizard of Oz*

William Rose Benét 1886-1950, Brooklyn. Pulitzer Prize-winning poet and author: *The Dust Which Is God, The Devil and Daniel Webster*

E. L. Doctorow b. 1931, NYC. Novelist: *Ragtime, Billy Bathgate*

Lawrence Ferlinghetti b. 1920, Yonkers. Poet: *A Coney Island of the Mind*

Alex Haley 1921-1992, Ithaca. Novelist: *Roots*

Bret Harte 1832-1902, Albany. Short-story writer: *The Luck of Roaring Camp, The Outcasts of Poker Flat*

Joseph Heller b. 1923, Brooklyn. Novelist: *Catch-22*

Washington Irving 1783-1859, NYC. Essayist and short-story writer: "The Legend of Sleepy Hollow," "Rip Van Winkle"

Henry James 1843-1916, NYC. Novelist: *The Turn of the Screw, Daisy Miller*

Robert Ludlum b. 1927, NYC. Mystery writer: *The Matarese Circle*

Bernard Malamud 1914-1986, Brooklyn. Pulitzer Prize-winning novelist: *The Natural, The Fixer*

Herman Melville 1819-91, NYC. Novelist: *Moby Dick*

James A. Michener b. 1907, NYC. Novelist: *Centennial*

Arthur Miller b. 1915, NYC. Playwright: *Death of a Salesman, The Crucible*

Joyce Carol Oates b. 1938, Lockport. Novelist: *A Garden of Earthly Delights*

Eugene O'Neill 1888-1953, NYC. Nobel Prize-winning playwright: *The Iceman Cometh, A Long Day's Journey Into Night*

Mario Puzo b. 1920, NYC. Novelist: *The Godfather*

J. D. Salinger b. 1919, NYC. Novelist: *The Catcher in the Rye*

Maurice Sendak b. 1928, Brooklyn. Children's author and illustrator: *Where the Wild Things Are*

Rod Serling 1924-75, Binghamton. Television and screenplay writer: *Twilight Zone* series, *Planet of the Apes*

Irwin Shaw 1913-84 NYC. Novelist: *Rich Man, Poor Man*

Neil Simon b. 1927, NYC. Playwright: *The Odd Couple, The Sunshine Boys*

Edith Wharton 1862-1937, NYC. Novelist: *Ethan Frome, The Age of Innocence*

E. B. White 1899-1985, Mount Vernon. Essayist and children's author: *Charlotte's Web, Stuart Little*

Walt Whitman 1819-92, West Hills. Poet: *Leaves of Grass*

Herman Wouk b. 1915, NYC. Pulitzer Prize-winning novelist: *The Caine Mutiny, The Winds of War*

Artists

Diane Arbus 1923-71, NYC. Photographer

Peter Arno 1904-68, NYC. *New Yorker* cartoonist

Arthur Bowen Davies 1862-1928, Utica. Painter, printmaker, and tapestry designer

Jules Feiffer b. 1929, NYC. Cartoonist, playwright

Helen Frankenthaler b. 1928, NYC. Painter

Edward Hopper 1882-1967, Nyack. Painter

George Inness 1825-94,

Newburgh. Landscape painter

James Ives 1824-95, NYC. Partner in the Currier and Ives team of popular print-makers

Rockwell Kent 1882-1971, Tarrytown Heights. Painter and illustrator

John La Farge 1835-1910, NYC. Landscape and figure painter

Roy Lichtenstein b. 1923, NYC. Pop Art painter

Grandma Moses 1860-1961, Greenwich. Folk painter

Barnett Newman 1905-70, NYC. Abstract painter

Frederic Remington 1861-1909,

Grandma Moses, folk painter, was born in Greenwich, New York.

Canton. Painter and sculptor of the Old West

James Renwick 1818-95, NYC. Architect

Larry Rivers b. 1923, NYC. Painter

Norman Rockwell 1894-1978, NYC. Illustrator

Louis Comfort Tiffany 1848-1933, NYC. Painter, decorator, designer of stained glass

Whitney Warren 1864-1943, NYC. Architect

Stanford White 1853-1906, NYC. Architect

Gertrude Vanderbilt Whitney 1875-1942, NYC. Sculptor

Composers, Concert and Opera Personalities

Maria Callas 1923-77, NYC. Operatic soprano

Aaron Copland 1900-1990, Brooklyn. Composer

George Gershwin 1898-1937, Brooklyn. Classical and popular composer

Leon Kirchner b. 1919, Brooklyn. Pulitzer Prize-winning composer

Beverly Sills b. 1929, Brooklyn. Operatic coloratura soprano

Social Reformers

Amelia Bloomer 1818-94,

Homer. Women's rights leader

Maggie Kuhn b. 1905, Buffalo. Founder of the Gray Panthers

Eleanor Roosevelt 1884-1962, NYC. First Lady, writer, lecturer

Margaret Sanger 1879-1966, Corning. Founder of Planned Parenthood

Elizabeth Cady Stanton 1815-1902, Johnstown. Leader of the woman-suffrage movement

Sojourner Truth 1797-1883, Ulster County. Abolitionist

Frances Willard 1839-98, Churchville. Founder of the World's Women's Christian Temperance Union

Business Leaders

Philip Armour 1832-1901, Stockbridge. Founder of Armour & Company— meat packers

Clarence Birdseye 1886-1956, NYC. Invented the quick-freeze process for food

Joseph Bloomingdale 1842-1904, NYC. Co-founder of Bloomingdale's department stores

Arde Bulova 1889-1958, NYC. Head of Bulova watch company

Ezra Cornell 1807-74,
    Westchester Landing.
    Organizer of Western
    Union telegraph company
William Fargo 1818-81,
    Pompey. Founder of
    American Express and
    Wells Fargo
Benjamin F. Goodrich 1841-88,
    Ripley. Founder of
    Goodrich rubber company
George Hormel 1860-1946,
    Buffalo. Founder of
    Hormel meat-packing firm
John D. Rockefeller 1839-1937,
    Richford. Founder of
    Standard Oil company
Thomas J. Watson 1874-1956,
    Campbell. Founder of IBM
    business machine company
Frank W. Woolworth 1852-
    1919, Rodman. Founder of
    F. W. Woolworth Company

Government Officials
Benjamin Cardozo 1870-1938,
    NYC. U. S. Supreme Court
    justice
George Clinton 1739-1812,
    Little Britain. Vice-
    President under Jefferson
Schuyler Colfax 1823-85, NYC.
    Vice-President under Grant
Millard Fillmore 1800-74,
    Locke Township.
    Thirteenth President of the
    United States
Ruth Bader Ginsburg b. 1933,

Franklin Delano Roosevelt at the wheel of his car in 1939, a year before he was elected to an unprecedented third term as president.

Brooklyn. Supreme Court
Justice
Charles Evans Hughes 1862-
    1948, Glens Falls. Chief
    Justice of the U. S. Supreme
    Court
John Jay 1745-1829, NYC. First
    Chief Justice of the U. S.
    Supreme Court
Frank Kellogg 1856-1937,

Potsdam. Secretary of State
and Nobel Peace Prize-
winner
Fiorello La Guardia 1882-1947,
    NYC. Reform mayor of
    New York City
Philip Livingston 1716-78,
    Albany. Signer of the
    Declaration of
    Independence

Franklin D. Roosevelt 1882-1945, Hyde Park. Thirty-second President of the United States

Theodore Roosevelt 1858-1919, NYC. Twenty-sixth President of the United States

Elihu Root 1845-1937, Clinton. Nobel Peace Prize-winning Secretary of State

William Marcy "Boss" Tweed 1823-78, NYC. Notorious leader of Tammany Hall and the political machine

Martin Van Buren 1782-1862, Kinderhook. Eighth President of the United States

Scientists and Inventors

Carl David Anderson b. 1905, NYC. Nobel Prize-winning physicist

Julius Axelrod b. 1912, NYC. Nobel Prize-winning biochemist

Gail Borden 1801-74, Norwich. Inventor of evaporated milk and juice concentrates

Leon N. Cooper b. 1930, NYC. Nobel Prize-winning physicist

Glenn Curtiss 1878-1930, Hammondsport. Aviation pioneer

George Eastman 1854-1932, Waterville. Photography pioneer

Gerald Edelman b. 1929, NYC. Nobel Prize-winning biochemist

Richard Feynman 1918-1988, NYC. Nobel Prize-winning physicist

Murray Gell-Mann b. 1929, NYC. Nobel Prize-winning physicist

George Goethals 1858-1928, Brooklyn. Engineer who built the Panama Canal

Robert Hofstadter b. 1915, NYC. Nobel Prize-winning physicist

Irving Langmuir 1881-1957, Brooklyn. Nobel Prize-winning chemist

Hermann Muller 1890-1967, NYC. Nobel Prize-winning geneticist

Marshall Nirenberg b. 1927, NYC. Nobel Prize-winning biochemist

John Northrop b. 1891, Yonkers. Nobel Prize-winning biochemist

J. Robert Oppenheimer 1904-67, NYC. Physicist who headed atomic bomb development

Burton Richter b. 1931, Brooklyn. Nobel Prize-winning physicist

Carl Sagan b. 1934, NYC. Pulitzer Prize-winning astronomer

Astronomer Carl Sagan is an expert on space exploration and has written several books on astronomy for a popular audience.

Jonas Salk b. 1914, NYC. Developer of polio vaccine

Julian Schwinger b. 1918, NYC. Nobel Prize-winning physicist

Hamilton O. Smith b. 1931, NYC. Nobel Prize-winning biochemist

Elmer Sperry 1860-1930, Cortland. Inventor of the gyroscopic compass

George Wald b. 1906, NYC. Nobel Prize-winning chemist

Rosalyn Yalow b. 1921, NYC. Nobel Prize-winning physiologist

Sports Personalities
Kareem Abdul-Jabbar b.1947, NYC. Basketball player
Bob Cousy b. 1928, NYC. Hall of Fame basketball player
Julius Erving b. 1950, Roosevelt. Basketball player
Whitey Ford b. 1928, NYC. Hall of Fame baseball player
Frankie Frisch 1898-1973, Queens. Hall of Fame baseball player
Lou Gehrig 1903-41, NYC. Hall of Fame baseball player

Kareem Abdul-Jabbar, professional basketball player, star of the Los Angeles Lakers.

Hank Greenberg 1911-86, NYC. Hall of Fame baseball player
Walter Hagen 1892-1969, Rochester. Five-time PGA golf champion
Red Holzman b. 1920, NYC. Hall of Fame basketball coach
Willie Hoppe 1887-1959, Cornwall-on-Hudson. Winner of 50 world billiard titles
Bruce Jenner b. 1949, Mount Kisco. Gold medal-winner in the 1976 Olympic Decathlon and 1976 Sullivan Award
William "Wee Willie" Keeler 1872-1923, Brooklyn. Hall of Fame baseball player
Sandy Koufax b. 1935, Brooklyn. Hall of Fame baseball pitcher
Bob Lanier b. 1948, Buffalo. Basketball player
Vince Lombardi 1913-70, Brooklyn. Hall of Fame football coach
John McEnroe b. 1959, NYC. Tennis player
John J. McGraw 1873-1934, Truxton. Hall of Fame baseball manager
Al Oerter b. 1936, NYC. Four-time Olympic gold-medal discus thrower
Joe Paterno b. 1926, Brooklyn. College football coach
Digger Phelps b. 1941, Beacon. College basketball coach

Mark Roth b. 1951, NYC. Professional bowler
Vin Scully b. 1927, The Bronx. Radio and TV sports announcer
Warren Spahn b. 1921, Buffalo. Hall of Fame baseball player
Gene Tunney 1898-1978, NYC. World heavyweight boxing champion

Entertainers
Don Adams b. 1926, NYC. Television actor: *Get Smart*
Alan Alda b. 1936, NYC. Movie and television actor: *M*A*S*H**
Alan Arkin b. 1934, NYC. Movie actor: *Catch-22*
Bea Arthur b. 1926, NYC. Stage and television actress: *The Golden Girls*
Lucille Ball 1911-1989, Jamestown. Movie and television actress: *I Love Lucy*
Anne Bancroft b. 1931, NYC. Movie actress: *Agnes of God*
Barbara Bel Geddes b. 1922, NYC. Stage, movie, and television actress: *Dallas*
Humphrey Bogart 1899-1957, NYC. Academy Award-winning actor: *The African Queen*
James Cagney 1899-1986, NYC. Academy Award-winning actor: *Yankee Doodle Dandy*
Art Carney b. 1918, Mount Vernon. Movie and

Alan Alda has starred in several films in addition to playing "Hawkeye" in the TV show M*A*S*H.

television actor: *The Honeymooners*

Billy Crystal b. 1947, NYC. Comedian and movie actor: *Throw Momma from the Train*

Robert De Niro b. 1945, NYC. Academy Award winning actor: *The Godfather, Part II* and *Raging Bull*

Bob Denver b. 1935, New Rochelle. Television actor: *Gilligan's Island*

Kirk Douglas b. 1918, Amsterdam. Movie actor: *Tough Guys*

Richard Dreyfuss b. 1947, NYC. Academy Award winning actor: *The Goodbye Girl*

Patty Duke-Astin b. 1946, NYC. Academy Award winning actress: *The Miracle Worker*

Peter Falk b. 1927, NYC. Television actor: *Columbo*

Jane Fonda b. 1937, NYC. Academy Award winning actress: *Klute* and *Coming Home*

Lee Grant b. 1931, NYC. Academy Award winning actor: *Shampoo*

Valerie Harper b. 1940, Suffern. Television actress: *Rhoda*

Danny Kaye 1913-87, NYC. Movie actor: *Hans Christian Andersen*

Burt Lancaster 1913-1994, NYC. Academy Award winning actor: *Elmer Gantry*

Michael Landon 1937-1993, NYC. Television actor: *Little House on the Prairie*

Penny Marshall b. 1943, NYC. Television actress: *Laverne and Shirley*

Lee Marvin 1924-87, NYC. Academy Award winning actor: *Cat Ballou*

Walter Matthau b. 1920, NYC. Academy Award winning actor: *The Fortune Cookie*

Ethel Merman 1908-84, Astoria. Stage and movie actress: *Call Me Madam*

Mary Tyler Moore b. 1937, Brooklyn. Television

actress: *The Mary Tyler Moore Show*

Carroll O'Connor b. 1924, NYC. Television actor: *All in the Family*

Anthony Perkins b. 1932, NYC. Movie actor: *Psycho*

Bernadette Peters b. 1948, Queens. Stage and movie actress: *Annie*

Rob Reiner b. 1945, NYC. Director, television actor: *All in the Family*

Mickey Rooney b. 1920, Brooklyn. Movie actor: *Andy Hardy* series

Telly Savalas 1926-1994, Garden City. Television actor: *Kojak*

Brooke Shields b. 1965, NYC. Model and movie actress: *The Blue Lagoon*

Sylvester Stallone b. 1946, NYC. Movie actor: *Rocky* and its sequels

Jean Stapleton b. 1923, NYC. Television actress: *All in the Family*

Maureen Stapleton b. 1925, Troy. Academy Award winning movie actress: *Reds*

Rod Steiger b. 1925, Westhampton. Academy Award winning movie actor: *In the Heat of the Night*

Barbra Streisand b. 1942, Brooklyn. Academy Award winning actress: *Funny Girl*

George Burns, comedian and actor.

Claire Trevor b. 1909, NYC.
Academy Award winning
actress: *Key Largo*
Jon Voight b. 1938, Yonkers.
Academy Award winning
actor: *Coming Home*

Singers
Joan Baez b. 1941, NYC.
Folksinger
Harry Belafonte b. 1927, NYC.
Calypso singer and movie
actor
Tony Bennett b. 1926, NYC.
Pop singer
Vic Damone b. 1928, Brooklyn.
Pop singer
Sammy Davis, Jr. b. 1925,
Brooklyn. Pop singer
Neil Diamond b. 1941,
Brooklyn. Pop singer

Arlo Guthrie b. 1947, NYC.
Folksinger
Lena Horne b. 1917, Brooklyn.
Pop singer
Billy Joel b. 1949, The Bronx.
Pop-rock singer
Carole King b. 1942, Brooklyn.
Folk-rock singer
Barry Manilow b. 1946, NYC.
Pop singer
Melba Moore b. 1945, NYC.
Disco singer
Lou Reed b. 1942, NYC. Rock-
and-roll singer
Neil Sedaka b. 1939, NYC.
Pop singer
Pete Seeger b. 1919, NYC.
Folksinger
Carly Simon b. 1945, NYC.
Rock-and-roll singer
Tom Smothers b. 1937, NYC.
Folksinger/comedian
Dick Smothers b. 1939, NYC.
Folksinger/comedian
Jerry Vale b. 1931, NYC. Pop
singer

Comedians
Steve Allen b. 1921, NYC.
Talk-show host
Woody Allen b. 1935, NYC.
Film actor and director
Milton Berle b. 1908, NYC.
Stand-up comedian and
television star
Mel Brooks b. 1926, NYC. Film
actor, writer, and director
George Burns b. 1896, NYC.
Comedian and Academy
Award winning actor: *The
Sunshine Boys*

Chevy Chase b. 1943, NYC.
Television and film
comedian
Rodney Dangerfield b. 1922,
Babylon. Stand-up
comedian and actor
Jimmy Durante 1893-1980,
NYC. Stage, television, and
film comedian
Jackie Gleason 1916-87,
Brooklyn. Television and
film comedian
Alan King b. 1927, Brooklyn.
Stand-up comedian and
actor
Chico Marx 1887-1961, NYC.
Stage and film comedian
Groucho Marx 1890-1977, NYC.
Stage and film comedian
Harpo Marx 1888-1964, NYC.
Stage and film comedian
Joan Rivers b. 1937, Brooklyn.
Television comedian and
talk-show host

Producers and Directors
George Abbott b. 1887-1995,
Forestville. Broadway
producer, director,
playwright
Peter Bogdanovich b. 1939,
Kingston. Film producer,
director, writer
Stanley Kramer b. 1913, NYC.
Film producer, director
Stanley Kubrick b. 1928, NYC.
Film producer, director
Paul Mazursky b. 1930,
Brooklyn. Film producer,
writer
David Merrick b. 1912, NYC.

Broadway producer
Joseph Papp b. 1921, Brooklyn. Stage producer, director
Harold Prince b. 1928, NYC. Broadway producer, director
Gene Saks b. 1921, NYC. Stage and screen director
Martin Scorsese b. 1942, Flushing. Film director

Musicians
Cab Calloway b. 1907, Rochester. Band leader

Peter Duchin b. 1937, NYC. Pianist and orchestra leader
Duane Eddy b. 1938, Corning. Rock-and-roll songwriter
Al Kooper b. 1944, Brooklyn. Founded Blood, Sweat & Tears
Herbie Mann b. 1930, Brooklyn. Jazz flutist
Shelly Manne b. 1920, NYC. Jazz drummer
Gerry Mulligan b. 1927, NYC. Jazz saxophonist
Bud Powell 1924-66, NYC.

Originator of bebop piano playing
Sonny Rollins b. 1930, NYC. Bebop saxophonist
Fats Waller 1904-43, NYC. Jazz pianist and composer

Other Personalities
William "Billy the Kid" Bonney 1859?-81, NYC. Outlaw
Mathew Brady 1823?-96, near Lake George. Civil War photographer
Agnes de Mille 1909-1993, NYC. Dancer and choreographer
Peggy Guggenheim 1898-1979, NYC. Art patron and collector
Bob Keeshan b. 1927, Lynbrook. TV's Captain Kangaroo
William Kunstler b. 1919, NYC. Lawyer
Mark Lane b. 1927, NYC. Lawyer
Shari Lewis b. 1934, NYC. Puppeteer
Jacqueline Kennedy Onassis 1929-1994, Southampton. Former First Lady
Mollie Parnis b. 1905, NYC. Fashion designer
Saint Elizabeth Ann Seton 1774-1821, NYC. Founder of the Sisters of Charity of Saint Joseph, a teaching order of nuns
Ed Sullivan 1902-74, NYC. Columnist and TV host

The Marx Brothers comedy team (left to right: Zeppo, Harpo, Chico, and Groucho), stars of stage and screen.

Colleges and Universities

There are many colleges and universities in New York. Here are the more prominent, with their locations, dates of founding, and enrollment.

Adelphi University, Garden City, 1896, 8,261

Alfred University, Alfred, 1836, 2,258

Bard College, Annandale-on-Hudson, 1860, 1,178

Baruch College (CUNY), New York City, 1968, 15,030

Brooklyn College (CUNY), Brooklyn, 1930, 17,218

Canisius College, Buffalo, 1870, 4,859

City College (CUNY), New York City, 1847, 14,783

Colgate University, Hamilton, 1819, 2,691

College of New Rochelle, New Rochelle, 1904, 2,445

Columbia University, New York City, 1754, 18,617

Cooper Union, New York City, 1859, 1,050

Cornell University, Ithaca, 1865, 18,450

D'Youville College, Buffalo, 1908, 1,650

Elmira College, Elmira, 1855, 1,076

Fashion Institute of Technology, New York City, 1944, 12,121

Fordham University, The Bronx, 1841, 14,612

Hamilton College, Clinton, 1812, 1,170

Hartwick College, Oneonta, 1797, 1,470

Hobart College, Geneva, 1822, 1,061

Hofstra University, Hempstead, 1935, 11,998

Hunter College (CUNY), New York City, 1870, 18,390

Iona College, New Rochelle, 1940, 7,397

Ithaca College, Ithaca, 1892, 6,058

Jewish Theological Seminary, New York City, 1886, 490

Juilliard School, New York City, 1905, 872

Lehman College (CUNY), The Bronx, 1931, 9,956

LeMoyne College, Syracuse, 1946, 2,403

The Vassar College campus in Poughkeepsie, New York.

Long Island University—Brooklyn Campus, 1926, 6,838; *C.W. Post Campus*, Brookville, 1954, 8,220; *Southampton Campus*, 1963, 3,616

Manhattan College, Riverdale, 1853, 3,616

Manhattan School of Music, New York City, 1917, 885

Manhattanville College, Purchase, 1841, 1,502

Marymount College, Tarrytown, 1907, 1,142

Marymount Manhattan College, New York City, 1936, 1,600

Nazareth College, Rochester, 1924, 2,673

New School for Social Research, New York City, 1936, 6,050

New York University, New York City, 1831, 33,973

Niagara University, Niagara Falls, 1856, 3,002

Nyack College, Nyack, 1882, 980

Pace University, New York City, 1906, 13,567

Pratt Institute, Brooklyn, 1887, 2,898

Queens College (CUNY), Flushing, 1937, 17,921

Rensselaer Polytechnic Institute, Troy, 1824, 6,839

Roberts Wesleyan College, Rochester, 1866, 972

Rochester Institute of Technology, Rochester, 1829, 13,004

Russell Sage College, Troy, 1916, 1,250

Saint Bonaventure University, Olean, 1858, 2,797

Saint Francis College, Brooklyn Heights, 1858, 2,099

Saint John Fisher College, Rochester, 1948, 2,401

Saint John's University, Jamaica, 1870, 18,813

Sarah Lawrence College, Bronxville, 1926, 1,255

Skidmore College, Saratoga Springs, 1911, 2,158

State University of New York at Albany, 1844, 15,168; *at Binghamton,* 1946, 11,966; *at Buffalo,* Amherst, 1846, 23,470; *at Stony Brook,* 1957, 17,233; *College at Brockport,* 1867, 7,994; *College at Buffalo,* 1846, 11,211; *College at Fredonia,* 1867, 4,889; *College at Geneseo,* 1867, 5,578; *College at New Paltz,* 1828, 8,141; *College at Old Westbury,* 1968, 4,200; *College at Oneonta,* 1889, 5,963; *College at Oswego,* 1861, 8,235; *College at Plattsburgh,* 1889, 6,161; *at Potsdam,* 1816, 4,579; *College at Purchase,* 1967, 2,494; *College of Environmental Science and Forestry of Syracuse,* 1911, 1,844; *College of Technology at Utica/Rome,* 1973, 2,550; *Empire State College,* Saratoga Springs, 1971, 10,000; *Health Science Center at Brooklyn,* 1858, 1,641; *Health Science Center at Syracuse,* 1950, 1,100;

Maritime College, The Bronx, 1874, 993

Syracuse University, Syracuse, 1870, 15,421

Union College, Schenectady, 1795, 2,309

United States Merchant Marine Academy, Kings Point, 1943, 1,001

United States Military Academy, West Point, 1802, 4,340

University of Rochester, Rochester, 1850, 9,539

Vassar College, Poughkeepsie, 1861, 2,272

Wagner College, Staten Island, 1883, 1,501

Yeshiva University, New York City, 1886, 4,899

Where To Get More Information
NY State Department of Economic Development
1 Commerce Plaza
Albany, NY 12245
1-800-CALLNYS
or 1-518-474-4116 from outside the 50 states and U.S. territories

Further Reading

New Jersey

Bill, Alfred H. *New Jersey and the Revolutionary War.* New Brunswick, NJ: Rutgers University Press, 1964.

Cunningham, John T. *This Is New Jersey.* 3rd ed. New Brunswick, NJ: Rutgers University Press, 1978.

Fleming, Thomas J. *New Jersey: A Bicentennial History.* New York: Norton, 1977.

Fleming, Thomas J. *New Jersey, A History.* Nashville, TN: American Association for State and Local History, 1984.

Fradin, Dennis B. *From Sea to Shining Sea: New Jersey.* Chicago: Childrens Press, 1993.

Kent, Deborah. *America the Beautiful: New Jersey.* Chicago: Childrens Press, 1987.

McCormick, Richard P. *New Jersey from Colony to State, 1609-1789.* rev. ed. Newark, NJ: New Jersey Historical Society, 1981.

Myers, William S., ed. *The Story of New Jersey.* 5 vols. New York: Lewis Historical Publishing Company, 1945.

Robertson, Keith. *New Jersey.* New York: Coward, 1969.

New York

Bliven, Bruce, Jr. *New York: A Bicentennial History.* New York: Norton, 1981.

Ellis, David M. *A History of New York State.* Ithaca, NY: Cornell University Press, 1967.

Ellis, David M. *New York: The Empire State.* 5th ed. Englewood Cliffs, NJ: Prentice-Hall, 1980.

Fradin, Dennis B. *From Sea to Shining Sea: New York.* Chicago: Childrens Press, 1993.

Pink, William B. *Getting to Know New York State.* New York: Coward, 1971.

Roseberry, Cecil R. *From Niagara to Montauk: The Scenic Pleasures of New York State.* Albany, NY: State University of New York Press, 1982.

Stein, R. Conrad. *America the Beautiful: New York.* Chicago: Childrens Press, 1989.

Numbers in italic refer to illustrations

Picture Credits

AP/Wide World Photos: pp. 29, 30, 31, 69, 70, 71, 72, 73, 74, 75; Bruce Glassman: pp. 4, 43 (right), 67; James Kersell: pp. 38, 39 (top); Jean McDougall: pp. 8-9; Courtesy of Museum of the American Indian: pp. 20, 58; Courtesy of National Portrait Gallery, Smithsonian Institution: pp. 24, 28, 59; Courtesy of New Jersey Travel & Tourism: pp. 3, 6, 7, 14, 16, 17, 18, 19, 22, 23, 27; Courtesy of New York Public Library/Stokes Collection: pp. 25, 60, 63; Courtesy of New York State Department of Economic Development: pp. 35, 36-37, 39 (bottom), 40, 41, 42, 43 (left), 44, 45, 46, 47, 48, 49, 50, 51, 52, 53, 54, 55, 56, 57, 61, 62, 66, 76; Jerry Pinkus: p. 11.
Cover photos courtesy of New Jersey Travel & Tourism and New York State Department of Economic Development.